TOTALLY SURROUNDED

With Danger On Every Side,
Would She Live To Fulfill Her Destiny?

CHRISTINA DI STEFANO DAVIS

PUBLISHING
A MINISTRY OF YOUTH WITH A MISSION
P.O. Box 55787, Seattle, WA 98155

YWAM Publishing is the publishing ministry of Youth With A Mission. Youth With A Mission (YWAM) is an international missionary organization of Christians from many denominations dedicated to presenting Jesus Christ to this generation. To this end, YWAM has focused its efforts in three main areas: 1) Training and equipping believers for their part in fulfilling the Great Commission (Matthew 28:19). 2) Personal evangelism. 3) Mercy ministry (medical and relief work).

For a free catalog of books and materials write or call:
YWAM Publishing
P.O. Box 55787, Seattle, WA 98155
(425) 771-1153 or (800) 922-2143
e-mail address: 75701.2772@compuserve.com
www.ywampublishing.com

Totally Surrounded

Published by YWAM Publishing
P.O. Box 55787, Seattle, WA 98155, USA

Unless otherwise noted, Scripture quotations in this book are taken from the Holy Bible, New International Version®, Copyright© 1973, 1978, 1984 by the International Bible Society. Used by permission of Zondervan Publishing House. The "NIV" and "New International Version" trademarks are registered in the United States Patent and Trademark Office by International Bible Society.

Some names have been changed to protect privacy.

ISBN: 1-57658-165-9

Printed in the United States of America.

This page-turner is so filled with excitement and adrenaline-producing escapades that halfway through the book you have to remind yourself that it's not a novel but the true story of a young woman who dared to follow God to a guerrilla-infested jungle. Not since *Through Gates of Splendor* was released have I been so personally challenged by a book about obedience to God—no matter where He called! I couldn't put it down. Every page brings the reader face to face with the thrill—and the cost—of following Jesus *completely*. You will laugh and cry as the heart of this story impacts your life—and you will end up knowing that *Totally Surrounded* should be read aloud to children and be required reading for teenagers and adults. This book should be purchased for every church library and Christian school in the country. This is the book that will make missionary biographies popular again.

Carol Kent, speaker and author of Tame Your Fears *and* Speak Up with Confidence (NavPress)

This is a book that every believer deserves to discover! What a story! Christina's story will transform your life! God will rekindle the fire of His Spirit in your heart and life as you read this gripping account of one saint's miraculous experiences in Christ.

Glenna Salsbury, president of National Speakers Association and author of The Art of a Fresh Start

This book will keep you on the edge as you read this true story of a nineteen year-old young woman who loves the Lord so deeply that she leaves all behind to go into the jungle of the Philippines for Him. Your heart will be touched by her sensitivity, warmth, and love. Christina's testimony is inspiring to young and old. Praise God for adventurous people like Christina Davis. A must-read book!

Judy Russell, wife of Bob Russell, senior pastor of Southeast Christian Church in Louisville, Kentucky

There is a saying, "The world has yet to see what God will do with a man (or woman) who is fully and wholly consecrated to the Holy Spirit." …You will be blessed as you see what God accomplished through a young woman who was wholly committed to His call.

Gary and Ann Marie Ezzo, founders of Growing Families International, a ministry to over one million parents

After having served as a close air support pilot of an A-10 aircraft in the Air Force and currently as an interior lineman in the National Football League, I can appreciate the sense of being in the trenches. This book must be read by anyone looking to be inspired by an individual's dedication and obedience to fight the daily spiritual battle of a Christian and follow the will of God.

Chad Hennings, defensive tackle, Dallas Cowboys

Christina Di Stefano Davis is an "impact player"—full of boundless energy and refreshing intensity and with a heart that beats for the little people. Here is first-century faith in the midst of twentieth-century tensions—deep in the Filipino jungles surrounded by the ruthless NPA communist guerrillas. Her story will strengthen your soul for your own battles.

Stu Weber, lead pastor of Good Shepherd Community Church and author of best selling Tender Warrior *and* Four Pillars of a Man's Heart

The incredible story of Christina Di Stefano Davis reminds us how God is at work in our lives—in extraordinary revelations and in everyday gentle whispers of assurance. *Totally Surrounded* touched my heart and left me with a deep longing to walk closer with Him.

Alice Gray, speaker and author of the million-copy seller Stories from the Heart

To my husband Michael for encouraging me
to serve God in the gifts He has given me.
Most especially,
for providing a loving family for me and our boys.

To my boys, Jake and Trevor:
There are things we cannot measure—
The depths of the deepest sea,
The stars up in the sky,
And the gift you are to me.

Laughter, fun, and adventure
Always fill my days.
The great love I have for you
I cannot count the ways.

A portion of the proceeds from the sales of this
book goes to support nationals in the Philippines to be
fully trained in Bible college for full-time ministry
and an orphanage home that takes care of
hundreds of homeless children.

To all of you who have bought this book,
To all of you who have made donations,
To all of you who are supporting a child monthly,
To all of you who are sponsoring a Bible college student—
thank you for supporting the ministries in the Philippines!!!

OTHER INTERNATIONAL ADVENTURES

❧ ❧

Adventures in Naked Faith

Against All Odds

Dayuma: Life Under Waorani Spears

Living on the Devil's Doorstep

The Man with the Bird on His Head

Tomorrow You Die

Torches of Joy

Contents

Foreword 9

Prologue 11

1. Locked Doors...17

2. Without a Map...27

3. What's Under My Bed?..41

4. A Way In 49

5. Jewels in the Jungle..53

6. View from the Mountain 61

7. Fever in the Night..67

8. A Deadly Banana Peel 75

9. Slippery Steps..81

10. House of Joy...87

11. Burning Bibles 97

12. A Dive into the Pit...103

13. A Narrow Escape 111

14. A Stranger Among Us...121

15. A Heart Left Behind 125

Epilogue..133

Afterword 143

Discussion Questions 145

Pictures..151

Foreword

This is an adventure story of almost unbelievable proportions. Consider the sheer audacity of it all: a young woman—still a teenager and barely out of high school—living in a communist guerrilla–infested jungle in a remote, previously unevangelized region of the Philippines. The pages of this book will raise the hair on the back of your neck as you read of the dangers this young woman faced. You will cry as you read of lives, young and old alike, being incredibly changed by the power of the love of God at work through the life of a young woman who definitely does not fit the commonly accepted profile of an evangelical missionary.

Christina Di Stefano Davis is a curious and courageous example of what can happen when a young life is simply and completely offered to the Lord—and what happens when He accepts the offering and says, "Come."

Pastor Jim Hayford
Woodinville, Washington

Prologue

The scorching sun beat upon my head like fire as the jungle began to swallow our small party. Several young Filipino men led the way through the thick bush; the other helpers walked behind, on careful watch for my safety. I could only imagine what kind of dangers surrounded me. I had been told about snakes and other inhabitants of the jungle floor that did not provide a pleasant welcome mat. I had been informed that certain bites or stings could be fatal. Most threatening was the rumor that the NPA (New Peoples Army) communist group, seeking to overthrow the government, was hiding out in the thick of these mountainous jungle regions. Oddly, the idea of encountering the NPA seemed far more remote to me than accidentally stepping on a snake's head.

For courage-boosting purposes I chose not to use the towering palm trees and bush grass as frames of reference; I focused on my Filipino guides. Although I was only five-foot-five, I felt like a giant compared to the Filipinos. Step by step I followed their dark-skinned, bare backs. In a daze at times, I listened to them speak in a language that was foreign to my ear. With my long, golden brown hair swinging against my back, I felt strangely out of place yet exhilarated by the opportunity I would have to share Christ with these people.

My helpers insisted on carrying what little I had: a few skirts, some shirts, one sweater, a couple of pairs of shoes, a few toiletries, a brush and comb, my Bible, and some first aid items. Since my arms were free of any load, I had a heightened feeling that I was soaring, free, completely given to God to do with as He wished. That feeling kept me moving when my body became tired.

It was hot and humid, and the thick air made it hard to breathe after walking so long. Every so often one of the men would climb a coconut tree to fetch me a drink. With ducklike feet clinging to the trunk, the man would scurry to the top and let as many coconuts fall to the ground as we needed. He'd then raise his machete and slice into the fruit, freeing the delicious buko juice inside. Picking up half of the coconut, I'd tilt it and let its juice run into my mouth. Every drop penetrated my thirst, and I desperately reached for more. If only it were cold, I thought. But at least it's a drink! I chided my spoiled, American taste buds.

We marched on for what seemed like miles until everything began to look and feel and sound the same: thick jungle, tall grass, birds singing and cooing, mosquitoes nipping—and who knew what else around each bend. The path was narrow but visible by day. In the thickest part of the jungle, the man walking in front of me reached for his machete and swung it left and right to keep the sharp grass from slicing my skin. When it began to get dark, all I could see was where to take my next step.

Where in the world am I? What am I doing here? Maybe I should have stayed home. My mind raced with questions, but a single thought reigned supreme: No man has the right to hear the gospel twice until every man has heard it once. The people in this region were unreached, and they had every right to have the opportunity to hear. I had vowed that a risk of my personal safety and comfort would not deter me from providing that opportunity.

Just as the stars were beginning to shine like diamonds in the sky, we reached a clearing at the edge of the jungle, and I could see the silhouette of a village in the valley below. In the distance, the ocean spread out as far as I could see, and several other villages were scattered along the shore. At the edge of the cliff, with the jungle behind me, I stood still and gazed at the land in front of me.

I closed my eyes and prayed, "Lord, what is now darkness, please make light. Lights shining for You. May I not leave here until there is praise being lifted from these people unto You."

❧ ❧ ❧ ❧

Everyone wanted to know the purpose of my visit, so word spread rapidly when the people discovered that the Americana was here to teach them about God. I quickly got to know the people as they came out of curiosity to talk to me.

About two weeks after my arrival, I was reading under a coconut tree in front of our hut when two girls came running down the dirt path shouting, "Ate [Aunt] Christina, someone is coming to see you." The girls hurriedly explained that a man from a more remote province had heard that I had come to help people understand how to know God, and he was coming to talk with me.

Full of excitement, I ran inside the hut to get my Bible and the chalkboard I had bought in Manila to help write out some simple explanations. Just as I was stepping back outside, a tricycle (a carrier balanced on a type of motor scooter that could hold several people) pulled up in front of our hut. A tall, slender man carefully stepped out. He leaned onto a cane and slowly made his way down the pathway to my hut. I walked up to meet him halfway. As a sign of respect, I took his hand in mine and placed it on my forehead. I greeted him in Tagalog, the primary language of the Philippines. "Hello. How are you? My name is Christina." I gestured for him to follow me to the yard.

"My name is Pay Job," the man said. "I have heard that you can help us know God better. I am anxious to know if you have a Bible."

"Yes I do." A warm smile came over Pay Job's face as I hurried into the hut. After rummaging through the bag of supplies I had purchased on a recent trip into Manila, I found a New Testament that Pay Job would be able to understand. As I walked back outside, my eyes met Pay Job's, and I knew God was at work.

Tears began to fall from his eyes as Pay Job told me his story. "When I was young, I went near to the city to stay with some relatives for a visit. While I was there, someone told me God had written a book to help us know Him better. It was called the Bible. I am now sixty years old, and I have waited nearly forty years to see this book." He gazed deep into my eyes. "Thank you for coming here. Thank you for this gift."

Sitting under the coconut tree that afternoon, we spent several hours talking. As Pay Job proudly held his own Bible, we read Scripture verse after Scripture verse of how God made a way for us to know Him. Using the chalkboard and an interpreter, I made simple diagrams to illustrate the points made in Scripture and translated a booklet showing the steps to salvation. After Pay Job had asked many questions and done much reading, God revealed the truths of Scripture to Pay Job's heart. Tears welled up in Pay Job's eyes as he listened to me. I asked Pay Job whether he understood what I was saying, and he nodded. I asked him to bow his head and repeat a prayer with me; then I led him through the prayer to give his life to Christ and to accept Jesus into his heart.

When we had finished praying, Pay Job looked up and said, "I did not choose Him, but He chose me. He chose to willingly come down from His comfortable home to live here on earth. He willingly chose to go to the cross to die for my sins. He chose to make a way to forgive me and make me clean. He chose you to come here to tell me about all these things. Now, I choose to give Him the remaining years I have on this earth to tell everyone in these villages about what He has done for us."

God had prepared Pay Job's heart long before I arrived. I wondered whether God had put it on other people's hearts to come here during the past forty years only to have the cares of the world keep them from coming. Or could it be possible that God knew as He prepared Pay Job's heart that it would be forty years before He would send such an unlikely person as me to be the one to lead Pay Job into the kingdom of God?

Locked Doors

Whoever finds me finds life and receives favor from the Lord.

Proverbs 8:35

I grew up in San Francisco, in a family with five children: four girls and one boy in the middle. We had some fun family gatherings and went on family vacations, but what I remember most about my childhood was the tension I felt between my mom and dad. My father turned to alcohol in an attempt to avoid their problems and soon became an alcoholic. By the time I was in grade school, I dreaded coming home. I knew I would have to listen to my parents scream at each other over and over again about the same things. At that age, I couldn't even imagine how bad the screaming and violence would get.

From early on, I felt extremely responsible for my father's happiness. My older sister Nan and I always seemed to be able to make him smile. It was the simple things that made him happy: bringing his slippers to him as he reclined on the couch after dinner, sitting on his lap, playing piggyback, going for a walk. We both felt that if we could keep Dad happy, he wouldn't get frustrated with Mom.

When I was growing up, my family attended church. As for me, I had no idea what it meant to have a personal relationship with Jesus. One time when I was seven years old, I got in trouble. I had a mouth that seemed quite disposed to causing problems. On this occasion, I didn't feel that it was my fault, and I was angry that I was always the one who seemed to be in trouble. I grabbed a book called *My Jesus Book* that my Aunt Judy had given me for my first Communion and went outside to sit on the back porch. The sun was warm, and its rays began to quiet my spirit. My anger began to turn into sorrow.

At that moment I hated everything about my life—especially the unfairness and the tension. I held the book in my hands and looked at the cover. I noticed it had a big picture of Jesus surrounded by several children. Jesus' hands gently cupped the face of one of the children as He gazed into her eyes. All of a sudden I felt warm, as if His hands were on my face. I heard a voice inside me say, "Christina, you are special to Me, and I will take care of you." The moment was over as fast as it came. But to this day, I remember that moment as if it just happened. It was the first time I heard Jesus calling my name.

Meanwhile, my parents' unhappiness grew. Sometimes my parents' fighting would get so loud that Nan would gather all of us into the third-floor bathroom and lock the door. We would sit on the floor, our arms wrapped around our legs, waiting for the storm to end. On one of these occasions, I thought, *Surely not all families act like this. Why do they have to scream at each other? Why can't they just get along? Don't they realize how it makes us kids feel when we have to lock ourselves in the bathroom for fear of being hurt? As soon as I can, I'm leaving this house. I don't know where I'll go, but I'm not staying here anymore.*

Just as my mind was racing with thoughts of escape, we heard a loud crash. It sounded as if the whole downstairs had collapsed.

Then a dreadful screaming began to shake the entire house. Nan stood and said, "I'm sneaking out to call the police. Keep this door locked, and do not open it for any reason unless you know it's me." Although we were reluctant to have her leave the room, we agreed.

A few minutes after the bathroom door closed behind Nan, a horrifying silence fell over the house. It was the kind of stillness that fills the eye of a hurricane, when you're not sure what damage there is or when the storm will start again. The torment of the unknown gripped us, and we were afraid to move or breathe.

Suddenly we heard Nan's voice break the stillness as she yelled at the top of her lungs, "Mom, get out of the house now!" We heard Nan scurry up the stairs, and we opened the door just wide enough to let her fall in before slamming it shut. Out of breath, Nan said, "I called the police, but before I could give them all the information it got quiet. I was afraid to talk. Maybe Dad heard me on the phone. I hid behind the door trying to see what was happening. I saw Dad coming up to the second floor, and I sat as still as possible. I was afraid he was coming to find me. Instead of coming into my room, he turned and went into his bedroom. I heard him open his drawer, pull out his gun, and cock it twice. Before I could think I screamed for Mom to run, and then I ran back upstairs!"

My younger sister was crying, but I was just plain angry. We all stared at each other, feeling as if the whole outside world had been destroyed and we were the only survivors. Was Dad going to kill Mom? Would he hurt us? Would he kill himself? He came from a family involved with the Mafia, full of deceit, anger, and bitterness. It didn't make any sense to us that we would feel as though he really loved us and then have explosions like this happen all too often. Everything was too confusing for my mind to figure out.

The police found us locked in the bathroom. No sign of our parents. *Five children, left alone again.* By this time, we were used to being alone. But the pain—I never got used to the pain. It jabbed me sharper and sharper each time. Nothing made sense to me. Later that night, the police found my dad and told him not to return home. Two days later they found my mother at her friends' house and brought her home.

Weeks later, I looked out the front window just as my dad drove up. As the knife inside me divided my heart between wanting to see him and wanting him to stay away, I said to Nan, "I wish we could just have a peaceful and happy family."

My dad walked in and gave me a hug. As I turned to shut the door, I noticed a police car waiting outside. My dad walked upstairs, and I went into my room and peeked through the doorway to see what was going to happen. My whole life seemed to crash right in front of my eyes when I saw my dad leave his room carrying two suitcases. Tears rolled down his cheeks as he walked downstairs and out to his car. I wanted to run after him and try to make him feel better. I wanted to hold him and plead with him not to leave. Instead I slowly slid down the wall and sat there in my room. I wept harder than I ever had before. My life was torn apart, but I hoped now there would be peace and quiet.

We were told not to speak to our father. Some of our relatives said he was dangerous. I was torn. I felt I was one of the few who cared for him, and yet everyone was filling our minds with terrible stories that made me and my brother and sisters afraid of him. The only way I knew how to cope with the conflict was to avoid it.

From that time on, I was basically on my own. I had no curfew and no rules. Freedom turned into bondage in the form of forced self-sufficiency and the absence of care. My only real moral guidance came from my older sister Nan, who at an early age had taken over the household responsibilities. If there was anything I could not take care of myself, I went to her. In many ways, she filled the empty places in my life. But she was four years older than I, and when she went away to college as soon as she graduated from high school, I knew I'd have to make my life work by myself.

I became very street smart. For most of high school I didn't see any reason to pursue an education beyond the survival lessons life was teaching me. My brother Jack and I became very close and often got into trouble together. We frequently cut class to go skiing for several days at a time or just to go to the beach for the day. One night when I was fifteen, I was at the beach with some friends and saw my dad's car parked at the other end of the lot. I sneaked away from my friends to see whether it was my dad. There he was, with his head in his hands, his sobbing audible over the sound of the ocean waves rolling in to shore. My heart felt ripped open again. I was forced to face the feelings that I had tried so hard to hide in a safe place. I still didn't know what to do with my feelings, myself, or my dad. I felt sure I was the only person who could make my dad feel better, but I was so afraid to go to him because of all the stories my relatives had told me about him. I didn't know what was true. I didn't know whom I could trust. I didn't know how to make anything right. I didn't go to him that night but decided to close that door and focus on what I could control and what I did know.

What I did know was how to ski. I skied more than I went to class. One time during my senior year, I had gone to Lake Tahoe for a week to ski. My mother telephoned me where I was staying. "Well," she said, "you've done it now. They won't let you back this time. Now what are you going to do?"

I had been expelled from high school. What *was* I going to do? That question nagged at me. But as usual, I had a plan. I was good at getting myself out of almost any trouble. I had to be. But as I looked around at my friends, my doubts grew. My friends were all older than I and out of high school already. Diplomas weren't pressing matters in their lives, but neither was having a purpose or living beyond momentary thrills. All of a sudden, I thought of my future. I became afraid of the unknown. I didn't want to be doing in another two years what I was doing now. Somehow I had to graduate.

When I got back from Lake Tahoe, I met with the senior counselor at the school I was attending, and we mapped out a plan of action. She asked every teacher to give me a certain amount of work that could be done by graduation, which was three months away. If

I met each requirement, I could graduate. My counselor had only one stipulation: I had to agree ahead of time to go to college. "College?" I said. "Are you kidding?" I thought it would be a miracle if I could graduate from high school.

My counselor took out a large map of California and showed me where all the junior colleges were. I asked, "Are there ski resorts near any of them?"

She looked at me and nodded. "There's one in Mount Shasta, which is five hours north of us."

I put a red pin on the map. "It's a deal. I'll go there."

I spent the next three months in the library. Up to that point I had never studied for a test, written a paper, or read a book. Now, however, I worked diligently and fulfilled all my requirements by the end of the three months. Every teacher passed me, except the nun who taught my English class. She insisted that the quality of the work was so good that someone else must have done it for me. My counselor knew the work was authentic because she had checked my progress. She fought for me, but the teacher would not budge. If she would not give me a passing grade, I could not graduate. My counselor told me to go to graduation as if I were graduating. She would appeal to higher authorities.

The big day came. I was excited, yet careful not to get my hopes up too high. I went through the whole procession, waited through the long line, and walked up onto the stage when they called my name. I took a deep breath and held my hand out to take my diploma. I was afraid to look inside the cover in case it was empty. I smiled and held the diploma all the way back to my seat. I knew my friends—as well as my family members who were there—were wondering. I had even sent a graduation invitation to my dad, hoping he would be there. I sat down and tried to act like everything was fine. I was good at that.

Nonchalantly, I looked down and opened up the bright red cover. My heart sank. It was empty. I felt so disillusioned. All that time studying, and for what? Nothing! What a waste! In that moment, the mess of my life seemed complete. My family was a mess, school was a mess, most of my friends were moving on to other things, and I didn't want to hang out with the ones who weren't. Scariest of all was the realization that what I did with my life was up to me, and I didn't know what I was going to do. The weight of managing life alone and the fear of how others could unjustly influence it without my permission began to squelch my belief that I could make everything turn out fine.

As we stood for the procession out of the huge Catholic church, I fought hard not to let my disappointment show. I was afraid I would burst out crying, so I bit my lip even harder. When we walked outside I saw my counselor running as fast as she could, frantically waving a big piece of paper.

"I've got it," she cried. "I've got it! It's a little late, but I finally got the principal to override the decision."

"Thank you!" I shouted. Looking into the eyes of one who saw more deeply into the hurts of my life than I dared to, I gathered strength from her hopes for me. I let go of all that built-up anxiety and found myself laughing and crying at the same time. That diploma gave me, in so many ways, an assurance that my life at least had some sort of direction, if not a well-made plan.

I kept my part of the deal and headed north in the fall. Looming some fourteen thousand feet above the plains and marshes of upper Northern California stands Mount Shasta. Awesome in its enormity, this remote sentinel of snow and granite has at its base— among other things—a college, and I was headed for it. With leaving home came a certain relief, but also a certain regret that I was not, as so many who go off to college, leaving the security of home. But I had been making my own way, and I could make it here, even if I had only a few bucks in my pocket. My girlfriend drove me up in her old yellow Volkswagen and dropped me off. I found a place to stay, got a job, stated nutrition as my major, and skied a lot. I worked in the school cafeteria to cover my living expenses and school costs.

Halfway through the second semester, I met a girl named Carolyn Testerman at the salad bar. We spent many afternoons talking in the cafeteria. One day Carolyn asked me a very strange question: "Are you on God's side or Satan's side? You can't be in the middle; you have to be on one side or the other."

Oh no, I thought, *not another one of those spiritual gurus. Of course I am on God's side.*

Then she said, "If you're on God's side, He calls you His special child. He will be your Father and always take care of you." Then she read a Scripture verse to me from her Bible: "Not everyone who says to me, 'Lord, Lord,' will enter the kingdom of heaven, but only he who does the will of my Father who is in heaven" (Matthew 7:21).

I listened politely but noncommittally, then went on about my work. Carolyn was persistent, though, and each week she invited me to her church. I was hesitant to go with her because I knew there were a lot of cults in the region, and I wasn't about to go to one of their meetings. I didn't want to go with her, but at the same time I could not stop thinking about what she had said. "If you're on God's side, He calls you His special child." *How do I know for sure that I am on God's side?* They were the same words I remembered hearing in my heart when I was seven years old sitting on my back porch.

I finally decided to go to church, but I went to a small church closer to my house that felt more familiar and safe. Maybe there would be something there that would help me know more about what Carolyn had said. Maybe I hadn't been old enough to understand it before.

It was a very cold winter. I wrapped up in my warmest coat and walked several miles on the icy, snow-packed roads to attend the tiny church that served the mountain community. The people were nice and friendly, but the service didn't seem particularly different from the masses I remembered from my childhood. I returned home, stoop-shouldered with the letdown that what I was looking for was not in that building. Carolyn's words about God being my Father and that I was special to Him reverberated in my mind. I looked up at the sky as if God were up there and said, "God, if You're real and I can know You somehow, please show me what to do."

The next Sunday I knew it was right to go to church with Carolyn. The little Calvary Chapel had twenty members. By the end of the service I sensed that these people knew more about God than I had yet seen or heard. I was curious and, deep down, hungry for what they knew. The pastor told me that God spoke to us today primarily through the Bible. He gave me one, and I devoured it.

One night in my room, about two weeks after I had started reading the Gospels, I reached the part where Jesus goes to the cross. All of a sudden I realized that He had done that for me and that He was waiting for me to come to Him so He could forgive me of my sins. Right there I knelt and accepted Christ into my heart and completely gave Him my life. I began to understand God as my Father and that I could have a real and personal relationship with Him and could rest under His care and provision. No more managing my life alone. I immediately recalled the incident when I was seven when God had called to me. The incident suddenly made sense, and I could look back at how He had cared for me all these years when I wasn't even aware of it. I couldn't believe I had lived so long without knowing the comforting reality of Christ as my loving Savior and Lord. I committed myself right then to tell others about Him.

Telling the rest of my family was not an easy task. At first, most everyone thought I was a bit strange. I started with a phone call to my father. It had been nearly three years since he'd left, and I had not spoken to him since that time. We met for an awkward lunch in San Francisco, trying to rebuild a relationship that had been badly shattered. It meant all the world to him that I made the attempt to contact him, but I was still not strong enough to face the pain he clearly carried. Though it was difficult for me, I continued to keep in touch with him and shared my newfound faith in Christ. Just a few months later, I received word that Dad was in the hospital with a massive heart attack. I spent several afternoons in his room playing songs on my guitar to try to cheer him up. It was not easy, but

it felt so good to have him back in my life. I never even imagined that after all this he would not make it. A few days later, his heart failed and he died. When I was cleaning up some of his things in his apartment I found a letter that he had started to write me. "My dear Chrissy, Thank you for the time we shared at lunch. I missed you more than words can tell...I love you, Daddy." What I had just worked so hard to get back into my grip had been torn right out again. I barely had him back and had lost him again. It was through this pain that God showed me He would be the Father I needed.

At the end of my second semester I decided not to return to Shasta but to instead enroll in Bible college in San Francisco. I wanted to learn more about the Bible and how to share the message of salvation with my family members and whomever God brought me into contact with. God showed me He does not waste any part of our lives. I had learned to be courageous under difficult circumstances growing up, but He was already turning that courage into use for His purposes.

CHAPTER TWO

Without a Map

'Come, for everything is now ready.'

Luke 14:17

At Bible college, my heart for sharing Christ was turned towards the unreached in remote areas of the world. Stories from my professors and required readings as an evangelism/missions major were causing me to picture the world differently. I imagined looking at the world through God's eyes and seeing the unevangelized corners of the world highlighted in yellow. I can still see Jim Albright, my missions professor, with his hand on his chin, shaking his head and looking at me with that "I don't know what to do with you" look. He suggested that I consider a short-term missions trip one summer to get some experience.

Until then I had been cramming in credits during all school breaks, including summer vacation, so that I could graduate as soon as possible. I was enthralled with missions. I had read dozens of books about what God was doing in remote areas and was fascinated by the courage that missionaries displayed. I was blessed to have several friends who felt the same way. We would meet at school at 6:00 A.M. to pray through the book *Perspectives on the World Christian Movement* edited by Ralph Winter and Steven C. Hawthorne. We challenged each other to memorize *From Jerusalem to Irian Jaya* by Ruth Tucker. We were anxious to learn as much as we could, and such challenges had the added benefit of helping us ace all our tests.

I absorbed the stories. We read about what God had done in the lives of Amy Carmichael, Elisabeth Elliot, George Müller, Hudson Taylor, David Livingstone, and others. Their examples deepened my faith. As they stepped out in obedience to fulfill God's plan for them, He was already going ahead of them to prepare the way. Reading these stories strengthened my determination to be a part of God's work on the mission field. I wanted to go where no one had yet heard the gospel, and I wanted to go where no one else was willing to go.

One day during a class break, I sat in front of our school building talking with a friend. As was often the case, we were discussing missions. "Christina," my friend asked, "why do you always want to blaze a new trail? When we go skiing, you always want to ski the side of the mountain that hasn't yet been skied. When we go to the beach, you're the first one to dive in the ocean when the waves look too rough. Now you want to go to some remote place to share God's Word. You're crazy! Why would you want to be in a situation like that when there are so many people here in the US who haven't heard the gospel?"

I hadn't considered that there was any correlation between my love of adventure and my vision for missions. I simply answered, "My desire for missions is not about the excitement or the risk. It's about giving someone the chance to know about God's forgiveness and new life through Jesus Christ. Sometimes I try to see the world from God's view. He sees the entire world. Here there are so many believers who can share the gospel. But what about the people who live in the absence of any Christian influence? Someone has to be willing to go to them."

I could see that my friend was trying to understand but was not yet convinced that this was God's best for me. "But," she said, "if you go, aren't you going to miss everything here? How long will you stay?"

"I'll tell you what," I answered. "If God does send me so far one day that I have no friends, no food, no clothes, and no fun, then you send me a package full of stuff that I love, okay? That can be your ministry to the remote regions."

We both laughed as we joked about all the fun stuff she would put in my package.

"Anyway," I added more seriously, "this isn't my home. I'm just passing through this place. If God can find me useful in His purpose for this world, I want to be available."

✒ ✒ ✒ ✒

While attending Bible school, I was part of a local church that had a heart for evangelizing various ethnic groups within the San Francisco area. I was in a group that organized campus evangelism, discipleship classes, and seminars on the topics we were learning in Bible school. I worked primarily with a group of Filipino girls. Every Tuesday evening we had a Bible study and time of prayer.

One night was different. Every time I prayed, I saw an image of Jesus surrounded by hundreds of people. Somehow I knew those people were in the Philippines. As I looked at Jesus, He was beckoning me. I knew He was telling me I would work with those people. That night when I went home, I found a long, white envelope on the steps outside my room. Noticing it was from the Philippines, I tore it open.

Greetings in the name of Jesus! I have been informed by my nephew, with whom you attend Bible school, that you may be interested in doing some foreign missions work. I have need of a woman to come for two to four weeks to help me with our discipleship classes. Would you please consider this opportunity? Write me as soon as you have a decision.

Pastor Calican

A rush of excitement welled up inside of me as I hurried to the phone. Calling my pastor, I explained the evening's events and asked what he thought I should do. The next day I told the news to my missions professor. Both agreed it would be a great opportunity. That day as I began to read my Bible where I had left off, I read Luke 14. " 'Come, for everything is now ready'" stood out in verse 17. I then decided to go to the Philippines for a few weeks in the summer. Since there were only three weeks of classes left in the spring term, I spent the time franticly taking finals and assembling what I need for my trip.

About that time, Billy Graham came to our area for a crusade. Several of my friends and I decided to rent a van and fill it up with nonbelievers to take with us to the crusade. We spent the day doing campus evangelism at a nearby city college, and by late afternoon we had filled all the seats in the van.

At five o'clock, I was heading toward the van to leave for the crusade. As I turned the corner of the last building before the parking lot, I saw the van, filled with my friends waving for me to hurry. Up on a hill to my right I saw a girl with long, dark hair sitting on the grass under a tree doing homework. The limbs from the tree hung low above her head, shading her from the warm sun as she studied.

As I glanced her way, a voice inside me said, "Go talk with her." I looked back down the hill to my left and could see my friends anxious for me to hurry up. But as I looked back up the hill, the voice said again, "I want you to talk to her." Signaling to my friends that I'd be just a minute, I headed up the hill to talk to the girl under the tree.

I reached the tree and slipped down to the grass as if I wanted to do some homework of my own. Looking over at the girl, I said, "I don't usually do this, but I had this feeling I should come talk to you. A bunch of us are heading down to San Jose for a Billy Graham crusade, and we have some more room in our van. Would you be interested in joining us?"

"I have heard of him," the girl said. "He teaches the Bible, right?"

"Yes, he does, and he helps us understand what the Bible says about having a personal relationship with Jesus Christ."

The girl, whose name was Lisa, told me that a friend had just sent her a Bible. Lisa had begun to read it but couldn't understand it and didn't know where to go for help. I could see that God had been at work in her heart and that she just needed someone to explain how to be saved. I spent the next twenty minutes walking her through the steps to salvation, and then she prayed with me right there under that tree to accept Jesus into her heart.

I was so excited about what we were discussing that I had forgotten about my friends at the bottom of the hill. When I looked down, they were all standing next to the van watching us, and I knew that they had been praying for us.

I turned back to Lisa. "Would you by any chance want to come with us to the crusade?"

Lisa smiled as she gathered her books together. "Why not?"

We all piled into the van. At the crusade, Lisa went forward at the invitation given by Billy Graham. We started a one-on-one discipleship time each week, and within one month, her entire family had also given their lives to Christ. They all became very active in our church and were instrumental in helping to start a Filipino congregation. The time we spent praying for their relatives still in the Philippines was a strong wind to my fire for doing mission work in the Philippines.

⁂ ⁂ ⁂ ⁂

At the end of the semester, my missions professor asked me to see him in his office. Much of the time he joked around with his students, but this time he didn't. When I entered his office I could see that he was very serious. He was sitting behind his desk instead of on the usual comfortable chair in the corner. Nervously I sat down.

In a week I would be on a plane for the Philippines. I thought maybe he was going to pray for me. Maybe he was going to tell me to settle down and not be too enthusiastic and not to expect to change lives overnight. I took a deep breath and listened to his words—words I will never forget.

"It's very evident to me and to your other professors that God has gifted you in several areas and that His hand is upon your life," Professor Albright said. "Listen to His voice: It will be still and quiet. Stay daily in His Word for yourself, not only for helping others. In all other situations I have advised my students to finish their education first, then go out. But you have had so much hands-on experience doing ministry here, and you've nearly finished your missions courses. I have complete faith that you are well prepared. If you want to stay in the Philippines through the fall, you can pick up your studies in the spring. If you're sure of His leading, follow."

He bowed his head and prayed for me, and then he said, "Now you go on and have a great time—and be careful!"

I walked out of his office with chills running up and down my spine. Part of it was from excitement, but most was from a sense that God was going to use me. I was taking a step out of the boat just as Peter had. Would I sink or walk? I was apprehensive yet full of faith to step out onto the water.

The next day I went to the ocean where I often had my quiet time. Since I had been a young girl, this had been my favorite spot. I climbed down part of a cliff, over a sixty-foot drop, to a little alcove that had been carved out of the side of the mountain by the winds. As far as I knew, no one else in the world knew about this spot, so it was mine alone. It was a haven, protecting me from the winds of life. I would spend hours there watching the waves crash in, one after another. That day I wrote in my journal:

I used to come here as a child to escape the tensions at home. Feeling completely empty inside, I would sit and let all the peace I felt from the warm sun and ocean mist engulf every part of me. It was the only peace I knew. Now I sit here at age nineteen, loving the warmth of the sun and the mist from the ocean, but today I can say with thanksgiving, my peace comes from within. I am anything but empty. I am full to the brim and overflowing.

God has given me hope when I used to despair. God has filled my heart with love when I used to hate. God has filled my heart with forgiveness when I used to be bitter. God has filled my heart with purpose when I had no direction. God has filled my heart with compassion when I never used to care. God has filled my heart with giving when I used to have nothing to give. God has opened my eyes spiritually when they used to be blind.

I think of the Scriptures: "No eye has seen, no ear has heard, no mind has conceived what God has prepared for those who love him" (1 Corinthians 2:9) and "Do not be anxious about anything, but in everything, by prayer and petition, with thanksgiving, present your requests to God. And the peace of God, which transcends all understanding, will guard your hearts and your minds in Christ Jesus" (Philippians 4:6–7) and "God looks down from heaven on the sons of men to see if there are any who understand, any who seek God" (Psalm 53:2).

I looked towards the horizon. The sun was beaming through the clouds in the kind of sunset you see in photographs. I thought about God looking down on the earth, seeing all His people at work doing what they can to share His Word. We are pilgrims here, passing through, and I want to invest my time here in whatever way my little life can best fit into His big plan.

I hoped my task would be to rescue a hidden people from an eternity without God. I told the Lord that day that if He could do something with me at the young age of nineteen, if in His search of the whole earth His eyes would settle upon me, I was all His. My only request was that He select a place where no one else was willing to go.

❧ ❧ ❧ ❧

Finally, departure time had come. I could hardly believe that my heart's desire was about to become a reality—a two-week missions trip to the Philippines.

Since none of my family really understood my decision to go, a few friends took me to the airport for my sendoff. I was thankful for the layover in Japan and had already arranged to have a Japanese girl I knew visit with me while I waited. I had led her to the Lord in the US when she was an exchange student. During the layover, we talked about her growth and where she was going to church and the friends with whom she had been sharing Christ. She wished me well, and then I was off again, refreshed by stories of changed lives.

When it was time to land in Manila, I looked out the plane's window and wondered what in the world I was doing. Had my adventurous spirit taken me too far? I wondered what the Philippines would be like. Since I had nothing with which to compare it, I had no idea of what to expect. But even from the airplane I could see how pretty it was. The land was covered with coconut trees and surrounded by waters not unlike that part of the Pacific Ocean that had been home to me.

The airport was total chaos. Huge crowds of people were shoving and pushing. I found myself caught in the midst of the stampede, unable to move. I had no idea where to go. I finally found a sign in English that read CUSTOMS in bright red letters, and immediately I headed for it. I waited in a long line for what seemed like hours. Everyone was talking rapidly, but I couldn't understand a word. I wondered whether I would make it out of the airport, much less find Pastor Calican.

Finally I got through customs and reached the outdoors. I was nearly trampled by the crowds coming and going. Hundreds of signs directed people to find whomever they were looking for. My eyes strained to read them as I was pushed to and fro. Then I saw it—*Christina Di Stefano.* Pastor Calican greeted me warmly and immediately led me to a jeepney, a minibus with open sides. The jeepney seats about five Americans on either side, but the Filipinos try to get at least ten on either side. Inside the jeepney, I met Pastor Calican's wife and daughter. I was so relieved to see them. I felt as though they had snatched me from a tornado.

My welcome to the Philippines was in a church in the middle of the city, which seemed appropriate, since the body of Christ here would truly be my home. When we drove up, people came running from all directions to greet me. The girls smothered me with kisses on my cheeks as the little ones climbed on top of me to give me gifts they had made. Pastor Calican had to peel the people off me so that I could walk into the church building. Once inside, I was overcome by the welcome they had prepared for me.

The church was old and run-down, but the people were rich in spirit. They were anxious for me to try the variety of Filipino foods that lined the tables: huge yellow pineapples, plump red mangos, papayas, bananas, and kiwis. Large plates were piled high with white rice that looked like mounds of snow. There was fried chicken with a strange-looking sauce on it. And a big bowl full of eggs. The young girls led me through the line introducing me to their favorite foods. They all began to laugh when we got to the bowl of eggs.

"*Balute!*" they screamed, doubling over with laughter. I could only imagine why they were carrying on like this. Had I said something funny?

One of the leaders of the church who spoke very good English came over to explain. "These eggs are called balute. They are eggs that have been fertilized and have a baby chick inside. They are considered a delicacy, and we offer them to guests as a special treat to show our appreciation."

I smiled politely. As they continued to introduce the foods to me, I couldn't help but hear the words of Professor Albright: "Be like them as much as possible. Eat what they eat, dress like they dress, learn their language...." The part about eating what they eat echoed in my mind, and all of a sudden I wondered whether coming here had been such a good idea after all. I might flunk this part of being a missionary, I thought. Maybe they'd let me make up for it by following the "dress like they dress" part well.

Later that night I reflected on my first impressions of Manila. Extreme poverty was the overwhelming image: open sewage that reeked in the streets, heaps of trash everywhere, and cockroaches the size of my palm running everywhere. Most of the buildings were run-down. Many people lived in tiny structures built of practically anything available—plywood scraps, cardboard strips, leftover roofing tin. For most Americans it would have been a terrifying sight. Despite my hearing about rampant gangs, robberies, and murders, I saw other things that gave me courage. Children played happily in the streets wearing nothing but underwear. Women and teenage girls walked without fear. Young boys played basketball in empty lots. If these people weren't afraid, I decided that I had no reason to be either.

I was overwhelmed by the friendliness of the people, who would wave and quickly send a greeting my way, surely wondering why I was in their city. My waist length golden brown hair and fair skin drew attention wherever I went. Children would surround me, reaching their dirty hands up to touch my face and hair. Most had never seen an American and believed my homeland to be a place of fairytales come true. I hoped to use their curiosity as a means of quick rapport.

Missionaries and churches had Manila widely covered, but little evangelistic work took place beyond the city limits. I was helping Pastor Calican with the youth in the church, but I didn't feel I was doing anything that anyone else couldn't do. I felt an intense pull to venture out of Manila, as if someone were calling me. It felt a little like the way the ocean pulled me when I was a young girl. The ocean would seem to call my name, and I would let loose and tear down the hill to the sandy white beach. This feeling was similar, a deep longing, but I didn't know where I was being called to.

"Pastor Calican," I said one day as I was nearing the end of my two weeks, "I would like to go to some of the unreached regions of the Philippines."

He laughed. "You aren't going any farther than where you are. It's dangerous in many places, and I need to watch out for you."

"But surely you know someone who could escort me," I said.

He shook his head. "It's too dangerous."

I knew I couldn't leave without his blessing, so I prayed that God would change his heart and provide a way for me if that was truly His will for me. During the waiting time, I decided to pursue other areas within Manila. Before I left the United States, Lisa, the Filipino girl I had met under the tree, had given me the address of a cousin by the name of Clarisa who was attending college in Manila. Lisa had never met Clarisa, but the two cousins had corresponded for several years. That afternoon I decided to find this cousin. It was the first time I had gone out into the city of Manila on my own.

After several jeepney rides, I arrived at the school Clarisa attended. The school and its adjoining board facilities were squished between other run-down business buildings on this busy and very dirty street. To my surprise, I was easily led to Clarisa's dorm. I walked up a dark, narrow hallway on creaky stairs that I felt sure would collapse at any moment. Reaching the top, I found three doors made of strips of plywood. Knocking on one, I called, "Is Clarisa here?"

The door opened, and I saw several girls sitting on mattresses on the floor doing their homework. A beautiful girl with big, dark eyes stood and said, "Hello. I am Clarisa."

When I explained that I was a friend of Lisa's, the girls all squealed with delight, making me feel like I was a famous movie star. They all drew close and started asking me questions so fast I couldn't even hear them. "Why are you here? When did you arrive? Where are you staying? How did you get here? Who is taking care of you?"

We talked for quite some time. I quickly learned that many of the Filipino girls love to be friends with "Americanos." They think America is the land of dreams. Clarisa couldn't understand why I would want to leave America to come to her land. We spent most of the afternoon together hearing each other's stories, and I caught Clarisa up on news of her family in America. Clarisa then accompanied me back to the church.

When I asked Clarisa when we could visit again, she said, "I am leaving tomorrow for a two-month school break. I will be going farther east into the province area to visit my family." Then she smiled and asked, "Would you like to join me?"

This was my chance to get out of Manila and explore other areas. "I will have to talk to Pastor Calican and see what he thinks," I said. "If he says yes, I would love to go with you!"

Together we went to the building where Pastor Calican was working. I explained to him the events of the day and my hopes to join Clarisa. He leaned back in his chair, looking worried. "If you go, how long will you stay?"

"Well, Clarisa has two months off from school. So maybe a week, maybe a month. I do not know. I only know that I have a deep desire to share God's Word with those out in the deep province area who have not yet heard the gospel. It is difficult for me to go back to the U.S. when I have an opportunity like this in front of me."

"I will interpret for her and accompany her everywhere we go," Clarisa said. "She is welcome to stay with my family, and they would all enjoy hearing about Lisa and her family from someone that knows them."

Pastor Calican straightened in his chair and asked, "What's your plan? When will you be leaving?"

"Tomorrow morning," Clarisa answered.

Pastor Calican looked at me warmly and said, "Well, you'd better get your things together. It looks like you're going to get to see the province area. You may go on one stipulation: that you phone me from Ilocas every week to let me know you're safe. Be careful— it is not safe to travel too far back into the province."

I jumped up and gave him a big hug. "We'll be all right, and I will keep in touch!" I was beginning to see God work in my life the way He had in the lives of the missionaries I had read about. I could not have predicted this route to the remote areas of the Philippines. But God was leading me, and I trusted completely what He was doing in my life. Little did I know then that my two-week trip was about to turn into months, then years, and then a lifetime ministry.

CHAPTER THREE

What's Under My Bed?

I will counsel you and watch over you.

Psalm 32:8

My hands reached out to grip the seat in front of me as I held on for dear life. The bus swerved to the left and then to the right. I thought I would fly right through the broken window. The bus driver obviously did not care about his life or the lives of those on board.

Turning to Clarisa, I asked, "How long did you say it would take to get to Ilocas, or wherever it is we are going?"

She smiled and answered, "Anywhere from eight to twelve hours. It all depends on whether the bus will continue on. Buses often break down, and we have to wait for another one to fetch us and take us on in the direction we need to go. Sometimes the driver decides to go in a different direction, and again, we need to wait for another bus to take us."

I couldn't help but laugh as I thought, *Okay, these people have no concept of being on a schedule. We might get there today, we might get there tomorrow. Oh my…dear God, please let us get there safely today.*

It seemed that God's help would be necessary to ensure our safe arrival because there were no rules of the road in the Philippines. Jeepneys and cars raced by maniacally. If there were lanes, no one stayed in them. If there were speed limits, no one abided by them. There was no such thing as pedestrian right-of-way. Even where there were crosswalks, they were no guarantee of safe passage. When there was a break in traffic, pedestrians ran. And they had to run quickly because the drivers weren't even thinking about slowing down. They didn't even stop at stop signs or traffic lights. I expected to see cars piled up on the sides of the roads. Somehow the bus drivers understood how to handle the chaos and keep their bus intact—if not maintained.

Though the bus we rode was the best bus line the Philippines had to offer and was the primary source of transportation, it was in worse shape than any bus I had ever seen. Graffiti covered it inside and outside. Stuffing and springs were bursting from the shredded seat covers. I sat with a cloth over my nose trying to avoid the odors of urine and filth. Every window in the bus was shattered or completely gone, letting in the hot, humid air that stuck to me like icing on a cake. It had to be 110 degrees. The flies and mosquitoes repeatedly attached themselves to my skin for a quick snack, leaving my arms and legs full of red bumps that itched like crazy.

How I longed for someone to turn a hose of fresh, cold water on me to cool me off. I began to feel sick from the jostling of the bus as it swerved to pass the vehicles in front of us. My heart hit the floor several times when I looked out the front window while the driver attempted to pass. He would race full speed ahead with a vehicle coming straight at us from the oncoming traffic. I couldn't figure out their rules, but at the very last instant, seconds before a fatal crash, one of the drivers would decide to swerve out of the way and let the other by.

I realized that my hands ached from gripping the seat in front of me. This wasn't the kind of adventure I would choose to "enjoy."

I thought, *God, I trust that You know what I'm doing right now and that You'll get me to my destination. And I know You are aware that heaven isn't exactly what I had in mind just yet.*

I decided to concentrate on the view outside my window to take my mind off the near-death experiences occurring within and without. I began to get a feel for the countryside. Hills covered with coconut trees lined the horizon. Lush green grass, dotted with vibrantly colored flowers, carpeted the land. The sky was a deep blue without a cloud in sight. Contrasting the richness of the land was the poverty of the people. Broken-down plywood shacks housed an entire family. Sometimes several shacks were bunched together, while others stood off by themselves. I wondered what the people did every day. Did they work? Where did they get their food?

All of a sudden the bus pulled over to the side of the road. I looked at Clarisa and asked, "Why are we stopping?"

Clarisa nodded toward the back of the bus. All of the men had gathered behind the bus to urinate, talk, and decide where the bus was going to take us. (I supposed that such bathroom facilities were one way to cut down overhead costs.) The men finally decided to get back on the bus, and we assumed that we were back on track.

About midday we stopped at a little town to have lunch. Rice, fish, and fruit were plentiful, and they suited me just fine. We finished eating in thirty minutes, but we had to wait for the driver to take his rest before we could get started again.

"How long is that going to take?" I asked Clarisa.

Clarisa shrugged her shoulders and replied, "As long as he wants it to."

Since there's nothing to do in the middle of nowhere, we sat under a coconut tree and talked. The flies swarmed around our heads, and the mosquitoes ate so much of me that I felt sure I would pass out soon from loss of blood. After about two hours, when there was still no sign of our driver, another bus pulled up. A couple of the men in the bus hollered for us to join them, which we did.

Just as I was beginning to think the ride wasn't so bad after all, the bus jerked and threw us out of our seats. I thought we'd hit a big bump in the road, but then I heard a loud explosion, and the driver pulled the bus to a screeching halt. Could it be an NPA attack? Everyone stood up and started talking loudly and so fast it made me dizzy. We were told to get off the bus, and warnings about "making examples of capitalists" floated through my head.

It turned out to be a flat tire.

Every direction I turned, all I could see was rolling hills covered with coconut trees. No sign of help. To reassure myself, I told Clarisa, "That's all right. It won't take too long to fix a flat tire."

Clarisa shook her head. "They have a problem. There is no spare tire, so we will have to wait here until another bus comes by."

As we took our bags off the bus, I took a deep breath and said to myself, *Well, she told me this was how it could be.* I just hadn't imagined it would really be so horrible. I thought, *Why did they drive these beat-up buses over these roads without a spare tire, anyway?*

The men lined up at the side of the road in a squatting position and talked about "stuff." I'm not sure they even cared that we were abandoned in the middle of nowhere. I started to feel vividly out of place. I was unaccustomed to such lack of control and timekeeping. The "sticking out" feeling was beginning to wear on me. I was much taller than all of the others. My long hair was pulled up in a clip on top of my head to get it off my sticky neck. I wore a brown, wraparound cotton skirt, a cream-colored short-sleeved cotton shirt, and a pair of brown sandals. I had chosen these clothes so I wouldn't stand out, but I don't think it would have mattered if I'd worn a bright pink pantsuit. I was definitely a sight to see for these people. I wondered whether I would get used to the staring.

We waited by the side of the road for over two hours before we waved down an approaching bus to help us. That bus took us to the last town we would come to before entering the more remote village area. As the bus pulled over to let us out, children came running from all directions. They screamed for us to stop. *"Para! Para! Para!"*

Crowds of children were trying to sell food carried on trays tied around their neck. Each child tried to push his or her way through to get close to us while trying to out-scream the others. It was pure chaos to me. The culture was so completely different—the countryside, the people, the poverty—and my journey wasn't over.

After the bus ride we transferred to a jeepney, which we rode to downtown Ilocas, where there were several small stores and a bank. This was to be the last view I would have of a town run with some government control instead of witch doctors.

Clarisa and I then transferred to a tricycle, which took us to a place called Banngi. This was the province area where her family lived. The farther we rode, the more I began to feel I was leaving the comfort of home for behind me. The roads became more and more narrow until we were solely on dirt. Scattered along the roadside were huts made of various materials, mainly plywood, nipa, and bamboo. In contrast to the songs of birds and the sounds of children laughing were the buzz and sting of mosquitoes and the smell of sweat and smoke. With each mile we traveled, I could feel more and more insects stuck in my hair. I was quite relieved when the tricycle dropped us off in front of a big marketplace. Several long wooden benches stood under a tentlike structure made of nipa to shield the food from the hot sun.

It was nearly dark by this time, and we still needed to walk about a mile to Clarisa's village, where we would finally rest. From the time we got off the tricycle until we arrived at the door of Clarisa's home, at least fifty children dressed in ragged shorts and walking barefoot followed us, calling out, "Americana!" They wanted to touch me and hear me say hello. Although I was exhausted, I somehow gathered the energy to talk to them. They were a perfect audience to try out some of the new phrases Clarisa had taught me on the bus. The children doubled over with laughter as I asked them their names in their own language.

The path we were on grew narrower as we walked towards Clarisa's home. Before I knew we were there, an older woman had come running out of a hut toward us shouting something I could not understand. She first embraced Clarisa with a huge bear hug and smothered her with kisses. Then she looked at me, and without any hesitation grabbed me into her embrace.

"This is my mama," said Clarisa, smiling. "She is anxious to know how I know you and why I have brought you to our village."

Clarisa's family welcomed me warmly. This particular village had electricity, so we had lights by which we made introductions. Her family offered a somewhat refreshing cleanup in a makeshift shower, and then we ate an evening meal cooked over coals at the back of the hut. That night I slept on a blanket on a raised bamboo bed frame. In spite of my exhaustion I was filled with so much excitement, thinking, *I'm finally where I'm supposed to be!* I knew this was where I wanted to stay, at least for the time being.

A few nights later as I was trying to sleep, I heard a loud noise in the distance that sounded like a terrible cat fight. As I lay there, the sound grew closer and closer. I got up and looked outside. The sound was indeed heading our way. In fact, it seemed to be coming down the center of the road in front of our hut. What in the world was it? I was quite frightened by the unfamiliarity, terror, sadness, and proximity of the sound.

I went over to shake Clarisa. "How can you sleep?" I asked. "What is that noise?"

Clarisa got up and came outside with me to look down the road. By that time I could see what was causing the noise, and Clarisa explained what I was seeing. About a hundred Filipinos were joined together in mourning over the death of a family member. The procession, which had begun at midnight, was led by men carrying the casket raised high on big sticks. The others marched behind the men, wailing loudly in complete unison.

It sounded scary when it was at a distance, and when it was right in front of me, I felt extremely uneasy. The people shouted chants I couldn't understand as they wailed and cried. Clarisa explained that they would march for five hours and then put the dead body in the front room of their hut for five days for all to see. This ritual was intended to ensure that the spirits would have plenty of time to transport the soul of the dead man to a safe place. The village witch doctor would come to the hut every day and put oils over the body and chant several rituals. The family members would do nothing but wail and scream the entire time. This was my introduction to the rituals of animistic worship.

I went back to bed amazed and saddened by what I had just seen. I could still hear the wailing in the distance, but just as I was about to drift off to sleep, I heard a loud shuffling noise in the room I shared with Clarisa. The noise seemed to be coming from underneath my bed. I called to Clarisa and asked her if she heard anything. She listened and said she too heard a strange noise. I jumped over onto her bed, and the two of us waited for a snake or some other creature to dash out from under the bed.

We were so tired from being awakened by the funeral procession that we began to laugh in spite of our anxiety. Finally, we heard a loud thud, and out dashed the biggest, ugliest rat I'd ever seen. It was as big as a cat. It headed for the window, and then out it went. It squeezed through a hole in the window the size of a softball. My heart was racing. We laughed for quite some time at how scared we were, frozen on her bed in the corner of the room. I had had my fill of excitement for the evening, so I sang some worship songs to help me fall asleep and asked for angels to watch over me.

How I got from my cozy bed in my safe home in California to a wooden bed in the province area of the Philippines, watching an animistic memorial and being scared by a cat-sized rat, was something I pondered that night. God had replaced the question "What's under my bed?" with a peace in my heart as I drifted off to sleep singing my favorite hymn, "His Eye Is on the Sparrow." I was sure that night that He was indeed watching over me, laughing sometimes, but ever protecting and preparing me. Little did I imagine what lay ahead for me.

CHAPTER FOUR

A Way In

Commit your way to the Lord.

Psalm 37:5

Two weeks turned into four, and four weeks into almost two months. The people learned much about the Bible, and I learned much about the culture. I had made huge steps in conquering the basics of their language. Clarisa brought many people to sit under the enormous coconut tree in front of our hut so that I could share with them about God and His Son Jesus. One day, after everyone else had left, Clarisa said, "I thought I knew God through the good spirits, but now after hearing you explain so much about the God who is in the Bible, I believe what you say to be true. I want to ask Jesus to live in my heart, and I want to help you tell others about Him."

I led Clarisa in a prayer of salvation and began discipling her. I also shared with her my strong desire to go deeper into the more remote jungle territories. I had no idea how to get there or even where they were. From my studies in Bible college, I knew that several villages in the eastern jungles of the Philippines were totally unevangelized. I felt pulled to go there and could not shake the feeling. I believed with all my heart that God wanted me to go.

Perhaps I had begun to feel pulled when I read a book about George Müller that had a great influence on me. George had a desire to start an orphanage but had no money. Several people discouraged the idea because of the lack of funds. George responded by saying, "I didn't think this up on my own. God put this desire in my heart. It is up to Him to provide the funds, and He will."

I felt sure that God had placed within me this compelling desire to go to the jungle. I had no desire within myself to live so on the edge. Clarisa had informed me that any village more remote than hers did not have any electricity or running water, and there were rumors of communist guerrilla activity in the mountains. No small deterrents, yet, if this was God's desire, I was willing to adjust my life however necessary to accomplish His purposes. He would surely provide the way.

One night I dreamed that I traveled a long distance in several types of vehicles, ranging from a jeepney to different versions of a tricycle. I was dropped off at a path leading into the thick of the jungle. A handful of Filipino people were there to lead me and assist me with my bags. We headed straight on the path and walked for hours. I had no idea where I was. Just when I thought we must surely be lost, we suddenly came upon a clearing. In front of me was the sea, spreading across the horizon as far as I could see. Directly below me was a village. A man was sitting in the middle of the village with one hand extended straight up to the sky. Coming down from the sky was another hand, almost touching the man's. I was between the two, standing in the gap. I knew that was where God wanted me to be.

The next day I told Clarisa about my dream. I felt God was leading me somewhere else. To prepare for such an opportunity, we went to the city (Manila) to purchase supplies. Since it was not a trip I relished making, I focused on the purpose behind it to buoy my spirits. We purchased Christian materials for people in Clarisa's village to study and enough materials to take with me into the deeper region if I was able to go.

Upon our return a few days later there was a jingle at the front door. One of Clarisa's cousins had come to visit. (Since there were no telephones and the mail system was slow in the provinces, this was how relatives kept up with each other.) Clarisa's cousin's name was Johani. After spending some time listening to Johani talk, I asked him what it was like where he lived. He explained that he was from a village farther east, a small village by the sea. I asked him if I could come along with him for a visit when it was time for him to return. Johani hesitated, but he said he would take me if Clarisa's family would allow it.

When I asked what they thought about the idea, they firmly said no before I could even finish my question. They were adamant in their view that it was too dangerous for an American woman to be traveling into that area. The New Peoples Army (NPA) had been steadily gaining notoriety for its efforts to overthrow the government. It was not in favor of Americans and had already killed three Americans in other parts of the country—primarily for publicity. Clarisa's family was very protective of me. They felt I probably shouldn't even be out as far as Banngi. I had been blessed not to have been confronted by the NPA in my journeys thus far.

The next day we talked again. Clarisa's family's opinion had not changed. In two days, Johani would be going back home. I prayed that God would open this door by having the family allow me to go if this was His timing and place for me. The day of Johani's departure came. I asked the family, "Wouldn't you like it if Johani and your other relatives could learn about God like you all have? That is why I want to go. Isn't it right that they have a chance to hear the message that will secure their eternity?"

"I will not take her all the way if we sense any danger," Johani said. "I think Mama would love to hear about our relatives back in the United States, and Christina can tell all about them. Also, I can bring many men from this village to help us on our journey."

Clarisa's mother paused and stared at me for a few minutes. "Yes," she said finally, "she may go, but bring her back if there is any danger!"

I could hardly believe it! I was excited and nervous at the same time. I knew I wanted to go, but I had no idea what to expect. I said good-bye to Clarisa, who would soon be going back to Manila for her schooling and would give Pastor Calican an update. I promised the others I would keep in touch. The willingness of the village men to escort us to Johani's village amazed me. I credited it to God's providence and my "fame" as an Americana.

The entire journey with Johani paralleled the dream I had had earlier that week. We walked deeper and deeper into the jungle until I thought we were surely lost. Several young Filipino men led the way through the thick bush, and others walked behind, watching out for my safety. It was hot and humid, the air so thick it was hard to breathe after walking so long. It was fully dark, and the stars were shining like diamonds in the sky when we reached a clearing. I could see the silhouette of a village in front of me. In the distance the sea spread out as far as I could see. Several other villages were scattered along the shore. I closed my eyes and prayed, "Lord, what is now darkness, please make light. Lights shining for You. May I not leave here until there is praise being lifted from these people unto You." God had provided a way in, and I would not be alone. I did not know about the threat of death that awaited.

Chapter five

Jewels in the Jungle

For where your treasure is, there your heart will be also.
Matthew 6:21

Darkness had settled over the valley, and my body was tired from my travels. My feet were swollen, and blisters shot pain across my whole foot. I realized I was also suffering from mild heatstroke. I was anxious to get to a place where we could rest, yet full of excitement to meet the people and see the village.

Johani took me down into the village of Paralam and to his home. As usual, I immediately had a crowd following me, calling out, "Americana, Americana!" When we arrived, Johani's family was very friendly and welcomed me warmly. They were eager to sit down with me and find out why I had come. Johani's eldest brother Danni seemed particularly interested in what I had to say. They all thought it strange, however, that a young American woman would want to come to live in the jungle just to tell people about God.

Since I was planning on doing much more than that, I described all that I had been trained to do. I wanted to help the people with both their physical needs and their spiritual needs. I had brought basic first-aid supplies to care for minor injuries. I was equipped to analyze their food sources and help them balance their nutrients for optimum nutrition. I had curricula to help teach young children to read and write. The people seemed a little overwhelmed by the services I offered but sensed my sincere desire to help.

I fell asleep that night feeling, beyond the pain and fatigue, that I was so very far away from home that it was almost impossible to believe. I lay there amazed that this night I would sleep inside one of God's yellow highlighted corners of the world—a place of extreme poverty by most standards, but rich in possibilities.

I spent the first several weeks growing accustomed to the area and meeting lots of people. I had a great deal of adjusting to do, but my stay in Banngi had been good preparation for the way of living I was to follow for the next few years. The valley had villages, called barrios, only two of which had electricity (Paralam was not one of them). In these regions, a village constituted a cluster of huts usually made of bamboo, nipa, and banana leaves. Most of the huts looked as though you could blow them over with one big breath. Nature would often do just that when a typhoon passed through. There was no such thing as a toilet; an outhouse was built away from each hut. There was no running water; all the water came from a well. To bathe I had to go to the well and take two buckets of water into the washroom, a one-room shack built of plywood scraps and covered with nipa, and a few feet away from the hut. To my dismay, the cockroaches went to the same place for their baths! During the wet season, I could have as much water as I wanted. During the dry half of the year, I could have only two buckets a day, and no more. I found it a challenge to wash and rinse my body and my hair with just two buckets of water, but I did the best I could under the circumstances.

I dressed like the villagers did, wearing a cotton skirt and cotton shirt and going barefoot, (I'd wear sandals or tennis shoes if I needed to walk a long distance.) I ate what they ate; the meals were quite similar to those meals shared in Banngi: a pile of sticky white rice and some kind of fried fish. Paralam, though, had a variety of fish because the sea was so close. The vegetables were always steamed, the rice boiled, and the fish fried. I also ate a lot of fruit. There was an abundant supply of fresh bananas (*saging*), pineapple (*pinya*), coconut (*buko*), mango (*mangga*), and papaya (*papya*). There was little variation in our meals, all of which we cooked outside over a fire. Not everyone was able to meet their family's nutritional needs, and occasionally children died of malnutrition or from improperly treated water.

 All the water had to be boiled before drinking, and even then it often made me sick. Sometimes it would make me ill for only a couple of days; other times the sickness would last up to a week or longer. I avoided the water as much as possible, receiving most of my fluids from coconuts, which I would chop in half and drink the juice from inside.

It was fun to watch the teenage children make a game over who could climb the buko tree fastest to get me a drink. The children tried to teach me to climb it, but without success. First of all, in their culture, all of the women wore either a skirt or a dress. That in itself caused a problem. And even when I managed to keep the fabric out of the way, I couldn't quite get my feet to stick in one place the way the others could. The Filipinos could whip up and down a coconut tree as if they had lizard feet.

Though they had very little materially, most of the people seemed quite happy. I was especially impressed with their family structure. The husband would go to work either fishing, hunting, or building. Most of the men in Paralam were fishermen or farmers working a small plot of land near their hut. A few worked for rice paddy owners on the village edge. (These occupations supplied the goods traded at the market held in the center of the village, which was open to all who could come. Most families visited the local village market once a week to buy or barter for the things they would need over the next week. Once a month or so they would visit the larger market shared by three or four villages.)

The wife cared for the home and took care of the children. The children loved to play. They were always running around skipping rocks or chasing each other in a game of tag. The sound of their play became one of my everyday comforts. It amazed me how much the children, who for the most part were well-behaved, respected their parents. Each family had a strong identity, and there was an obvious respect for age. Because these were multigenerational families under one roof, authority issues were clear-cut, and every person in the family had a special place and role to fulfill.

The only unusual members of the household were the lizards. They were like household pets, and they were everywhere. They lived on the walls of each hut and attached themselves like glue to the ceilings. I kept waiting for the time when one of them would let go and fall on my head. Thankfully, it never happened, but it was quite an adjustment to get comfortable around the little creatures. Not only did they give me a creepy feeling, but they made loud yelping noises that made it difficult to sleep.

The appearance of such uninvited guests became common occurrences, like one morning not long after my arrival in the village. I had gotten up early and gone to the sea to prepare for the day. What a wonderful gift it was that God had brought me to a place next to the ocean to share His Word. I loved to sit by the water to have some quiet time with Him. Watching the waves roll into shore against the backdrop of the blue sky somehow almost transported me back to my own little hole by the sea in San Francisco. Everything else was so different and new, but this was one of the few familiar sensations I felt.

This particular morning my quiet time was interrupted by the sudden appearance of one of the little girls. She was running toward me, screaming my name. "Ate Christina, come quickly!"

I jumped to my feet. "What's the matter?"

"Come quickly. Mama Ayette wants to see you!"

I ran with her back to our hut. The women all gathered around me, looking me up and down. *What was going on?*

Mama Ayette explained. "We have found a centipede under your bed and are fearful it may have bitten you in the night. The ladies are looking to see if there is any change about you. Do you feel the same as you did yesterday?"

I nodded. "I think I do." How was I supposed to know how I felt? I didn't know anything about centipedes. Was I going to die? And would it be slow or sudden? I ran to get a book I had brought with me called *What to Do When There Is No Doctor.* There wasn't much on centipedes, except that there are different kinds. The ones found deep in the jungle can be deadly because they carry a certain kind of poison. The book said that in most cases the victim dies soon after being bitten. Since I felt fine, I wasn't too worried.

Secretly, I hoped that the book was talking about the jungles of Africa or South America. I had enough concerns adjusting to life in the Philippines without worrying about centipedes. I had to get used to bugs crawling on me at night, bugs crawling all over the walls while I ate, bugs just about everywhere. I had to get used to the fact that lizards, rats, and roaches were my constant companions. I had to get used to no electricity and no running water. Most important, I had to get used to the people's religion so that I could understand both what and why they believed what they did and how to respect their culture. I tried to learn their customs to avoid offending them, and I continued to learn their language. I had books to help me, but I mainly learned by pointing to things and listening to the people talk.

Living in a barrio made me feel as though I had been picked up and taken back to a time long ago. It was everything I had imagined it would be when I dreamed of being a missionary—and then some. I had to make Matthew 10:39 my own: "Whoever finds his life will lose it, and whoever loses his life for my sake will find it." I had to lose my life. I had to let go of wanting to be comfortable. I knew that if I was to have any chance of winning these people to Christ, I would have to empty myself of the customs and culture that I had grown up with and adapt to their lifestyle.

Sometimes I longed to sleep in my own bed in my roach-free home in California, have an ice-cold glass of clean water, go skiing, wear a pair of jeans, speak in my own language to someone who understood me, or get in my car and be somewhere in five minutes instead of walking for miles in the hot sun. Yet I always came back to something I had written in my journal when I first arrived in the Philippines.

When God plants a dream in my heart, that becomes my purpose, my focus and what I gather all my energies to achieve. I used to think that sacrifice meant giving up or not being able to do things I really wanted to do. Sacrifice to make my dreams come true is not a negative, but a positive. It allows me to clear the clutter in my life that would stand in my way of being and doing what is God's best for my life. My life must be held before God with an open hand. If I desire to fulfill God's will for my life, regardless of the price, I must give myself completely to Him. I want to live my life in such a way that when and if I grow old, I can look back and say: "I did not hold back from God, I gave Him all of myself as best as I could have done. He did that and more for me."

If my life were my own I would be doing what was comfortable and fun. When I gave my life to Christ, I made a decision to lose my life to find it in Him. My priorities were no longer my own but His. And the most pressing claim that I knew He had was for these people in this jungle area to know that He loved them and that He had died for their sins so that He could forgive them, establish a relationship with each of them personally, and bring them home to heaven when they died.

Elisabeth Elliot once wrote, "The willingness to be and to have just what God wants us to be and to have, nothing more, nothing less, and nothing else, would set our hearts at rest, and we would discover the simpler the life the greater the peace." So I pressed on, trying to serve in this world while storing up treasures for the next.

ﾟ ﾟ ﾟ ﾟ

The first several months I stayed around the one barrio of Paralam, spending most of my time learning the language and the culture. I was forced to learn Tagalog if I wanted to communicate, since few barrio dwellers spoke any English. The people were excited that I wanted to learn their language. Everywhere I went, they would point to things and say the word, then wait for me to repeat it. As I repeated each word or phrase, they would double over with laughter. For someone who likes to be encouraged, this was not very inspiring. But after some time, I learned to make it a game and laugh with them, because I knew deep down it meant a lot to the people that I wanted to communicate with them. With much rehearsal, in about six months I was able to speak "Taglish," which is half Tagalog and half English. In the meanwhile, I had an audience any time I wanted because they all loved to hear me talk or, should I say, attempt to talk.

Some days their amusement at my expense was unnerving. I often became exasperated trying to manage the word order, which was completely backward from English. If I wanted to say, "I would like to eat some food," in their language, it would be, "I food would like some eat." Whenever I grew frustrated, I would stop and find something fun to do. I had brought a Frisbee from the US, and I loved to take a few people out to an open field and let the Frisbee soar. I was pretty good at tossing it hard and long. The villagers would squat in a row and stare in awe at my ability. I would laugh inside and think, *I can't figure out your sentence structure, but I can throw a good Frisbee. There is something I know how to do!*

I'd point to one person at a time to come and give it a shot. You would have thought I was asking them to throw a flying saucer.

They would stand there apprehensively and hold the disk just long enough to get it out of their hands and into the air. Then laughter would fill the place and echo off the mountainside. After they tired of Frisbee, I would take groups into the jungle and teach them how to play hide-and-seek. To set boundaries, we tied long strips of nipa around the trees. The rule was that they could hide anywhere within the nipa. Most of the people never did catch on; they played the game more like tag. A person would hide way up in a banana tree, and then as someone passed below, he would fly through the air and pounce on his prey.

Sometimes I thought it was funny. Other times I wanted to scream, "You are doing it all wrong! You have to play by the rules!" I finally gave up trying to get them to play by my rules, and I just played by theirs. That was when I would feel that tap on my shoulder and hear the still small voice whisper, "That's your ticket!" I recalled what Dr. Albright had said in class, "The greatest problem in missions history has been when goodhearted men and women have gone to serve God in another culture and forced their culture on those to whom they were going. If God calls you to go, become like them. Then you will win their respect and trust; then you will be able to lead them to your Savior."

This was just the beginning of what God had planned to do in shaping me and bringing clarity to the eternity He had placed in the hearts of these people. I came to understand that my days of adjusting and building were the treasures God would have me rejoice in. The lessons in endurance, surrender, and humility, while not new ones to my life, were precious jewels finding a new shine in the Philippine sun. God was polishing and unveiling treasures in those around me as well. I prayed for eyes to recognize and praise them and for hands to uncover the hidden treasures.

Chapter Six

View from the Mountain

Commit to the Lord whatever you do.

Proverbs 16:3

That first season in Paralam I poured my life into teaching about fifteen people who had made solid decisions to follow Christ and who wanted to learn more. I began with Johani's oldest brother. I somehow knew when I first met Danni that God had something good in store for him. God had already prepared his heart; Danni had just been waiting for someone to come and show him the way. He had gone to Manila for part of his education and had been exposed to some biblical truth, but no one had explained it in enough detail for him to understand it. Once he did understand it, Danni had a zeal to know God and tell the others in the village about Him. He invited friends over to talk, and we started our first Bible study. I met with each person for one-on-one Bible time, and twice a week we met as a group. My days were busy as I prepared Bible studies, shared Christ with those who would listen, learned the language, and completed chores such as washing clothes and preparing food.

As the demands on my time and skills grew, I decided I needed an extended time of prayer. One day I ventured up to the top of a hill where I could have some quiet time alone. I was wearing a dark green cotton skirt that one of the women had brought me from another village. The skirt, which was longer than the others I had, worked well for walking through the bush, protecting my legs from the sharp grass. I also was wearing knee socks, tennis shoes, a sleeveless cream-colored cotton shirt, and sunglasses, and I had pulled my long hair on top of my head to get it off my neck. With my green skirt and cream shirt, I'd blend right into the scenery, and nothing would bother me. Into my backpack had I stuffed my Bible, notebook, journal, some fruit, and a bowl of rice.

I left without telling anyone where I was going because I wanted to be by myself. The village people never let me out of their sight. I could barely go to the washhouse without ten of them following me. I was in desperate need of some time alone without someone watching me. I wanted to have time to sit and just think, talk to God, and pray. As I walked the two miles through the bush up to the spot where I wanted to sit, I sang some of my favorite hymns. I felt as if I were living in a dream, that I was not really in the Philippines at all. Here I was, walking through a jungle to pray on a hilltop about the people God had brought me to. I looked ridiculous, was unsure about my safety, and was in desperate need of a friend. Nonetheless, I was energized with the task at hand and would give it my best.

Reaching my spot at the top of the hill, I turned to get a bird's-eye view of the entire valley. I could see for miles. The eight villages within my sight, built along the sea and backed up against the jungle, had tremendous needs. I could easily spend every waking hour taking care of just basic first aid. The people had no medicine at all. A simple insect bite would get so bad that it would swell several times in size. Applying simple antibiotic ointments was a huge help.

My mind raced with ideas concerning all that I could do and how I could most effectively spend my time. These people had so many needs that I wanted to help them meet. I asked God to help me know what to do first and to how to organize my time accordingly. I had been feeling pulled in so many directions that I wasn't doing anything well.

After praying, I wrote down all that I sensed God wanted me to do and made a list of the people's needs. Then I made some short- and long-term goals to meet those needs. I based the short-term goals on what I could get started on right away and what was most important. I based the long-term goals on a timeline that I thought would be sufficient for the people to learn how to accomplish the various tasks themselves. My goals were the following:

- To establish trust among the people so that they would be open to my sharing the gospel with them.
- To continue to learn the language.
- To witness in every village to as many people as possible.
- To disciple every new convert in four levels of growth.
- To establish a weekly Bible study to meet in each village and to establish at least one village church where everyone would come together on Sunday for worship.
- To train leaders through the discipleship program who could oversee all of the ministries that would be established.
- To establish a first-aid station and train someone to manage it.
- To establish an educational program for children ages five to ten that would help them learn to read and write.
- To establish trained workers at the marketplace to help the people with their nutritional needs.
- To train indigenous workers to run every ministry so that if I ever had to leave suddenly, my labor would not be in vain.

I then made plans for getting started on the most important goals: evangelizing the entire valley and establishing the discipleship training program. Foundational to those would be winning the trust of the people by doing what I could to meet their physical needs. As I prayed, I could hear Pastor Calican's words, "What's your plan?"

After quite some time in prayer and writing out my goals, I began to feel clearer. I was overwhelmed with trying to do everything and carrying the burden of it all alone. In my time of prayer, God spoke to me through these Scripturess: "All a man's ways seem innocent to him, but motives are weighed by the Lord. Commit to the Lord whatever you do, and your plans will succeed" (Proverbs 16:2–3); "Many are the plans in a man's heart, but it is the LORD's purpose that prevails" (Proverbs 19:21); "Trust in the Lord with all your heart and lean not on your own understanding; in all your ways acknowledge him, and he will make your paths straight" (Proverbs 3:5–6).

God put everything back into perspective for me. I was refreshed knowing that even in my planning, God would direct me. As I made myself available, He would be the one doing the work through me. As I was getting up to head back to the village, I took a last look over the entire valley. I prayed the words I had often spoken since first coming here, "Lord, what is now darkness, please make light. Lights shining for You. May I not leave here until there is praise being lifted from these people unto You."

A few days later two girls came running to tell me that a man was coming from another village to speak to me. Pay Job had come from the island of Tagaya and was the first to give his life to Christ from that island village. This was the beginning of how God led those people to Himself. I began to spend much time on Tagaya helping Pay Job share his newfound faith with the people of his village. Many people gathered to listen to us, mainly because of Pay Job's age. Pay Job was greatly respected in that area by everyone.

Pay Job arranged for me to speak in the courtyard several times a week to all who would come, while he translated for me. Many came at first out of curiosity, but soon had accepted Christ and were coming back to learn more. Pay Job and I continued to meet every day for one-on-one discipleship and I began another Bible study for those who were regulars at the courtyard.

After two months, a strange thing happened. One day, during our regular time in the courtyard, only a few people showed up. There was a stillness in the air—no crowds of children gathered around to see the Americana speak. I learned that the local witch doctor was angry that people were coming to me instead of to him. He told the people that I had bad spirits that would hurt them if they came to hear me. *You've got to be kidding!* I thought. How could these people be so easily intimidated? I didn't pause to think about any harm that might come to me by offending the witch doctor, and nothing would stop Pay Job from learning.

That incident only strengthened Pay Job and a handful of the others. It confirmed for me the need to focus on individual growth, not crowd appeal. I felt strongly that the harvest of a few deeply rooted believers would be greater than the shallow planting of many converts. I concentrated on deepening Pay Job's knowledge of the Scriptures. Pay Job eventually led his wife and two children to the Lord and witnessed the truths of Scripture to hundreds more. His enthusiasm was contagious and his zeal never-ending. His fear-less consistency in following Christ drew many past their fear of the witch doctor's curse into full fellowship with Christ. I was sure that God had led me to the island of Tagaya not to win many but to win one who would in turn win many.

As more decisions were made for Christ, I began to organize a discipleship school. Because the people did not operate very well by the clock, it was not an easy task. I became more flexible, and the people tried to come on time—whatever that meant to them. If I said to show up after lunch, that could be one o'clock or before bed; either way, it was after lunch. The people did not live by a set of rules or by the clock. Something else, something subtle that I hadn't yet figured out governed their ways.

I developed a four-stage Bible study plan for all new converts with the help of two small booklets I had brought with me. When an individual gave his life to Christ, he was immediately baptized. This solidified his decision right away. Then he was taught how to share his faith with his family and friends and was encouraged to do so immediately. Then he would go with me or someone from stage four on hut-to-hut evangelism in one of the other villages. After that he was encouraged to come to a stage-one Bible study group, which taught the basic Christian doctrines. He would then graduate into stages two, three, and four. Finally, when he had finished stage four, he would take on leadership responsibility in an area in which he felt gifted.

These key verses were written into the workbooks:

"Not so with you. Instead, whoever wants to become great among you must be your servant, and whoever wants to be first must be your slave—just as the Son of Man did not come to be served, but to serve, and to give his life as a ransom for many" (Matthew 20:26–28).

"Whatever you do, work at it with all your heart, as working for the Lord, not for men, since you know that you will receive an inheritance from the Lord as a reward. It is the Lord Christ you are serving" (Colossians 3:23–24).

I tried to keep the big picture in mind at all times so that I knew where I was heading when the day-to-day duties seemed to overwhelm me. I tried my best to be consistent and to make my life an example of what I was teaching. I tried to be the kind of person I wanted the new believers to be. That is not to say that I did not have some very frazzling days, but I was aware that people were watching me, and that was the main way they were learning. It made me grow in my own life because I was always striving to be a good example for others to follow. Individual obedience and consistency were sentinels of light on the path to following God's plans for my life and this region.

CHAPTER SEVEN

Fever in the Night

Consider how we may spur one another on toward love and good deeds.

Hebrews 10:24

Ate Christina, *magmadali! Tulong!*" hollered Mama Ayette.

The bucket slipped from my hands, and water splashed into my face. "I'm at the well," I called. "What is it?"

Out of breath, Mama Ayette rounded the corner. "Hurry! I have been to another village, and a boy is lying with high fever."

Looking up at the darkening sky, I realized it was going to start pouring any minute. With typhoon season here, we could get ourselves in a mess going that far from home at a time like this. But I ran into my hut to fetch the bag that contained my first-aid items, my medical book, and my umbrella. I slipped on my tennis shoes and took off with Mama Ayette down the dirt path.

Along the way Mama Ayette tried to give me what few details she knew about the boy. "I was visiting Nana Bising when we heard the woman in the hut down the road holler for the witch doctor. We ran to the hut to find the boy lying down with a hot head, not even wanting to sit up for a drink. I convinced the woman to call for you and not the witch doctor. After taking another look at her boy, she agreed, begging me to hurry. That is all I know. I came right away to find you."

It took us about thirty minutes, running the whole time, to reach the boy. All that running on the beach as a girl had prepared me for the endurance I needed so often here. The entire way there, I prayed that God would give me wisdom to know what to do. It always felt much easier when they called me when someone had only scratched his mosquito bites too much and they started bleeding. I would give the person some antibiotic ointment and cover up the wound with a bandage. All would be well in spite of my lack of extensive medical knowledge. I was wondering what I would do if this was malaria or something else serious, and how would I know whether it was serious or just the flu? I had put a Band-Aid on someone, and now I was expected to heal the people of all their diseases! I tried to make it clear that I was not a doctor, but that didn't matter to these people. In their eyes, if I could make something stop bleeding, it was as good as having a medical degree.

We arrived at a small hut, half of which was hanging over the water's edge. The hut was built on a hill alongside the calm part of the sea. It was made from nipa and banana leaves and looked ready to fall over. The father gestured for me to come in.

Once inside, I looked into the sweetest little face I had ever seen. Never before had I seen such big brown eyes. Pauli was seven years old. He was sitting on his mother's lap looking up at me as if I were an angel. His dirty little body lay limp. I spoke Tagalog to him to try to find out how he felt. His temperature was 104 degrees, and he was very pale, but he was able to answer my questions, and his reflexes were good. I looked for everything my book told me to look for and check out; then I gave Pauli some medicine for his fever. I also gave him a sponge bath and asked someone to get him a clean shirt. Then I laid him in his bed—a bamboo mat on the floor covered with nipa to make it soft. I told the family that I would stay with them until Pauli's fever came down and that I thought he would be all right.

I asked the parents if I could pray for them. When they said yes, I asked Pauli's father to hold Pauli in his arms. I asked God to please take care of the boy and to take away his fever soon. I left Pauli to rest and then sat with the parents, making small talk. The father told me he had no work and was trying to find something. He explained to me that he didn't have enough money to properly feed his five children and that he feared it was his fault that Pauli was ill. It burdened me to know that so many went hungry every day and that it would take less than a dollar a day to feed an entire family with at least some rice and bread. I sent for food for Pauli's family right away so that they would have enough food for at least the next few weeks. It was good to be able to help, but it always left me with a sick feeling. *What will they do after that? What about the little children next door? How do you help some but not others?* These were haunting questions—ones I knew I could not answer. I chose instead to focus on what I could remedy.

Since I had been welcomed into their hut to help their son, I felt I had earned the right to share with Pauli's family about Jesus. I explained to them that God knew them and that He had a plan for their lives. I explained about His sending Jesus to die for our sins, making a bridge for us to get to God. I spent over an hour slowly explaining the salvation message as they all listened attentively. I asked Pauli's father first if he would like to pray with me to receive Christ as his Savior and Lord. He nodded. I asked him to repeat after me as I prayed a simple prayer guiding him to receive Jesus into his heart. When we were done, he looked up at me with tears streaming down his cheeks and said, "Thank you" over and over. Then I had the entire family sit in a circle and hold hands. I helped the father lead the rest of his family in the same prayer. This was the beginning of a work being established in that village.

I stayed with them for the better part of a day until I could tell that Pauli was getting much better. It was the blessing of God that whatever was causing Pauli's fever proved to be only a minor problem.

❧ ❧ ❧ ❧

Such opportunities to heal seemed to go a long way in opening windows in which to share Christ. The most effective way I knew to earn the people's trust was to be as much like them as I could. Second was to help with the people's first-aid needs. The village people often called me "Doctor Christina." Anything pertaining to an illness or injury was traditionally the witch doctor's territory. In most cases, the people were only given a bunch of hocus-pocus from the witch doctors and sent on their way. When they came to me, I was usually able to help them get better.

In time, more and more people became brave enough to call for me, especially when it had to do with their children. Many times when I was able to help someone with simple first aid, it set off a fire of anger from the local witch doctor. The witch doctors became very angry and jealous when they saw that I was beginning to help the people. They felt threatened. News began to spread that I was a bad spirit and that the people should fear for their lives if they allowed me into their homes. Having been with these villages a significant length of time, I had established trust with many of the people. Although many knew that what I was doing was good, I was constantly attacked by those who were loyal to the witch doctors.

It was frustrating to have several people come to Bible studies and be very interested and then all of a sudden stop coming. In almost every case, they were scared off by the witch doctor or the gossip of those who had been spreading wild stories. It was such a battle. It felt as though every time we took two steps forward we would get pushed back four. That made me even more determined to gear up and get ready for battle, and yet we would be defeated again and again.

Sometimes I would get discouraged and wonder whether I would ever be able to make a difference. I knew I had to stay focused on the goals and keep on at a steady pace. Working at a slow and steady pace had never come naturally to me. I had to learn how because it was the only way to make it here day after day. The goals I had were impossible to accomplish overnight. The plan was for the long haul—maybe several years. I was on my own. I had no one to relieve me if I needed a break and no one to encourage me to keep marching on. It was me and God.

I was lonely at times and missed the fellowship of being with my friends, but somehow in the midst of all I was doing, it wasn't that important. I felt I had grown up ten years in one. I was learning lessons about trusting in God's provision and guidance that were deepening my relationship with Him. It was not just what He was doing in the hearts of the people but also what He was doing in me. He had plans for all of us; we were all growing together.

The discipleship school was growing, and the opportunity for us to reach the other villages began to open up. Many of the people were very comfortable around me, even if they did not yet know Christ. They had observed over time how I helped at the marketplace, treated many people who had injuries, and brought clothing for the children. The discipleship class had begun to reach out in several of the villages as our discipleship plan advanced. Many were growing in the Lord, and many new people were coming to faith in Christ. As I continued to build relationships among the village people, I especially emphasized the importance of trust among believers. I wanted those who had become Christians to have a deep understanding of what it meant to trust one another.

I felt we were getting attacked enough from the outside by untrue stories from the witch doctors. I encouraged a very high standard in our communications with one another. We were only to talk highly of one another. It's easy to find faults in others but harder to find the good that is there. We all tried to set our minds to look for opportunities to encourage each other. I told them that looking for the good in each other was like building a strong fence around us that no arrow from the enemy could penetrate.

I wanted to instill in the people that Christians are like family. They needed to be able to trust each other. I told them that if they were to tell stories that were not true, they would be taking away a very strong piece of bamboo that held our fence together and giving the enemy an open hole to tear us apart. I taught them the wisdom of Proverbs 15:4, "The tongue that brings healing is a tree of life, but a deceitful tongue crushes the spirit." From the start we all grew together like a strong force to conquer the remaining villages for Christ.

When back at my home base of Paralam, I liked to take walks down to the sea. The outstanding view—blue waters stretching out into the horizon reflecting the last rays of sun—set a mood of thanksgiving. On quiet evenings I loved to sit and listen to the waves crash against the shore. The ocean has always had a way of calming my racing mind and allowing me to better hear that still, small voice. There I would give myself, the people, and all my plans over to the Lord. I approached every day with this mindset. I often reminded myself that God first found these people, then He found my willing heart, and He matched us together to accomplish His will. He had a plan for these people and for me. Trusting one another was shadowed only by our trust in Him.

I know that God knew I needed something that particular morning. As I ended my quiet time and picked up my Bible to head back to the village, a piece of paper fell from my Bible to the ground. I leaned over and picked it up. It must have been stuck between the pages. I was about to put it back into my Bible when I noticed it was not in my handwriting. The note read:

> Every day just do the best you can. Try as much as you can to be like them. Earn their respect before you can expect to change lives. Let them make their own decisions and let them make mistakes. Make your quiet times a priority, and God will guide you. If I know you, you're gonna have fun.
> Jim Albright

I was completely overwhelmed. God knew exactly what I needed to hear. That note had been stuck in my Bible for over two years, and yet it happened to slip out just that morning. Jim Albright must have stuck it in my Bible before I left. God knew I would need it that day. Here was the pat on the back I needed, the voice that said to keep on marching!

Chapter Eight

A Deadly Banana Peel

You alone are the Most High over all the earth.

Psalm 83:18

The day was hot and muggy, but the market was bursting with activity as the sound of bartering filled the air. I loved to go to the market and see all the fresh supplies of fruit and vegetables laid out on tables. I would barter with goods I had purchased in Manila or had brought with me from the States. I was adept at bargaining by this time but still had to suffer through much amusement at my expense over my pronunciation and sentence structure. I was familiar with most of the fruits, even though the people often brought me something I had never seen before. But the vegetables were all very different from the vegetables with which I was familiar. I was very curious and asked a lot of questions. The market people loved to hear me talk. It was funny to watch them gather when they saw that I would soon be at their table.

As I moved from vendor to vendor, usually the most talkative person would carry on the conversation with me as the others stared, not missing a word. I enjoyed throwing the people off a bit by asking one of the observers a particular question. Often the person would just laugh and look to the speaker to answer me. The longer I was there, the more the people relaxed around me, but even when I became more fluent in the language, they would still laugh when I talked.

This day I had a large bag filled to the brim with all the fruits and rice I had purchased and was just ready to leave when I felt someone tugging on my bag. I turned to see a little girl staring at me. Her big brown eyes made me immediately break into a smile.

"I do not feel well," she said.

I put my hand on her head to feel if she was hot, but her skin didn't feel much warmer than normal. I put my bag down and lifted her up. "What is your name?"

"My name is Rosselle."

After asking her several more questions I found out that she was six years old and that she lived on the island of Madras. She had heard that I could make people feel better, so she had followed me around the market until she could find the courage to approach me. I told her I would first need to talk to her mother or father, but she said that they were not with her. She had come with her aunt, who was on the far side of the market. Rosselle had been told to wait by the banana table, where we were standing, until her aunt returned.

I told Rosselle that I would stay with her until her aunt came back. I held her on my lap the whole time. Rosselle was the sweetest little girl, with big brown eyes and shiny black hair that came down to her waist. While I talked to her I played with her hair, tying it into a braid to get it off her neck. When it got too hot in the sun, we found a place in the shade to try to cool off. I had someone fetch Rosselle a cold drink and did my best to examine her as we sat and talked.

I never helped a child without first going to the child's parents for approval. This was first out of respect, and second, to assure their trust and eliminate any chance of offending them by helping their child. If their ties were strong to the witch doctor and I helped the child without approval, there could be terrible consequences for the child, the parents, and me.

I could tell that Rosselle was running a low fever and that her upper respiratory tract was congested. She had a hard time breathing through her nose and had a cough deep within her chest. I told her that I would be able to help her, but I would first need to talk to her parents. She invited me to come to her home, and I accepted.

As we waited for her aunt, I told her lots of stories. I told Rosselle who I was and why I had come to live here. I told her all about who Jesus is and what He did for her. I told her that Jesus could come into her heart and live there, always by her side. But she couldn't understand how Jesus could get into her heart and, if He was inside her heart, how He could be by her side at the same time. Taking her sweet, little, dirty hand in mine, I placed it on her heart and said, "Remember, Rosselle, all you need to do is ask, and Jesus will always be with you and always take care of you."

Just about that time, Rosselle's aunt walked up and abruptly took Rosselle's hand, yanking her off my lap. When I tried to talk with her, she would not listen. She kept on walking. I hurriedly followed, trying to keep up. "Rosselle needs some medicine, and I can help her!" I cried.

The woman stopped long enough to say, "Rosselle has gone to the witch doctor, and she will be better. We do not need you. Leave her alone!"

I tried to explain, "She has a fever and a cold, and I have medicine that can make her much better."

The woman turned around one last time and said, "Rosselle was playing with the spirits and harmed one of them. She will not get better until she makes it up to the spirit she harmed. The spirit is angry with her. Only she can make it better. You can do nothing."

I stopped and watched as they walked away. Rosselle's frightened eyes connected with mine as she placed her hand upon her heart and patted it a couple of times. I smiled, her message clear. Still, I sat down angry, frustrated, and sad. Rosselle's eyes were piercing my heart. She left in silence, but her eyes were screaming, *Please help me!*

What had the aunt meant by saying Rosselle was playing with the spirits? I asked one of my friends to try to find out what had happened. Apparently, after Rosselle had eaten a banana the day before, she had thrown the peel by the side of the hut. Normally she would have thrown it in the garbage pile, which would later be burned. Rosselle hadn't thought anything of it, since it was only a banana peel, and had tossed it haphazardly aside.

Soon afterwards Rosselle told her mother she was not feeling well. Her mother took her to the witch doctor. After hearing Rosselle tell how she'd spent the day, the witch doctor told the child that she had hit a spirit with the banana peel when she threw it where it was not meant to go and that the spirit was now very angry with her. Rosselle was told she must appease the spirit by offering it a portion of her food for that day. He said she must put the food outside her hut at bedtime. If it was gone in the morning, she could assume the spirit would probably let her alone and she would feel better. Then the witch doctor said a round of chants, and off they went.

The next morning, the food was gone. The mother assumed that Rosselle would now be better, so she let her go to the market, which is where we met. Not only did Rosselle not feel better, but she was also weak from not eating. When she and her aunt left me, they returned home. Rosselle was still not better, so they returned to the witch doctor. They were told to repeat what they had done the night before. "Maybe she hurt one of the bigger spirits, and it will take more to appease it," he said.

That night they again put out what little food they had. They knew no other way; they believed they had to make a sacrifice to be saved from the wrath of the evil spirits. That night Rosselle went to sleep feeling worse, from sickness and hunger. The next morning, the food was again gone.

I asked one of the women to check on Rosselle and ask her parents if I could help her. Rosselle's parents said they wanted to let me help but were afraid. The witch doctor had told them that if they let me help, the spirits would be even more angry and would do them worse harm. By the third day, Rosselle had gone from having a low-grade fever, cough, and nasal congestion to being extremely hot and limp. At least that was how my friend described her condition to me.

That afternoon I went with my friend to Rosselle's hut, hoping I could convince her parents to let me see her. They would not come out of their hut. They were stuck between wanting me to help their daughter and believing that I could, and being frozen with fear that worse would happen if they allowed me into their home.

The third night they again offered all the food they had. Rosselle went to sleep that night for the last time. The idea of losing an innocent child because of ungrounded and primitive fear broke my heart. I had done all I could. I prayed that Rosselle had remembered my words to her, "Jesus will always be with you."

Later that night I prayed, "Please, dear God, let there be no more banana peels."

CHAPTER NINE

Slippery Steps

In all things God works for the good of those who love him.
Romans 8:28

After the loss of Rosselle, I became concerned that my battle to bring light to this place would fall to the powers of darkness the witch doctors possessed. It seemed time to dig trenches and to enlist the help of powerful people to do so.

Every barrio had a captain. The captain was something like a mayor, but on a much smaller scale. The people of the village were careful to treat the captain and the witch doctor as equally important. While the witch doctor handled mainly physical illnesses and spiritual concerns, the barrio captain handled civil concerns.

Since it did not seem likely we would get past the witch doctors' influence, the other believers and I began to pray that God would give us favor in the eyes of the barrio captains. I especially had my heart set on Rosselle's home, the island of Madras. It would be our newest target.

I chose one of the young men who had just made it through stage four in the discipleship school to join me. His name was Bobby Aldea. Bobby was like a little brother to me. He was with me more than the others and protected me from more harm than I knew I was capable of getting into. He was my shield, a tool in God's hands to make my paths straight in more ways than one. He accompanied me on several of my journeys throughout the jungle region and on longer trips into Manila to get supplies.

Together we mapped out the island of Madras and planned our strategy. Our first stop was the home of the barrio captain, Mr. Pann. It was about a five-mile walk through the thickest part of the jungle to where we could cross the water to the island. The sun was especially hot, making the hike tiring. I often wondered whether there could possibly be a better route, but I trusted Bobby to find the safest way there and back. The grass was over my head most of the time, so Bobby walked in front of me with a machete to clear the way. The grass was so sharp that I had to wear thick socks and a long skirt to keep my legs from getting sliced. A cut from the razor-sharp grass would bleed terribly. The snakes in the grass were also very dangerous, so we had to keep an eye out for any strange movement or noise. Unaware of the heavy NPA (New People Army) presence in this area, I believed that snakes were my only real concern.

Since I did not know this area and couldn't see anything but Bobby's back, I just followed. *This is how it is with God*, I thought. He leads one step at a time. I thought of how God promised to make my paths straight and to lead me: "If the Lord delights in a man's way, he makes his steps firm; though he stumble, he will not fall, for the Lord upholds him with his hand" (Psalm 37:23-24). Bobby saw his niche in the world as seeing to it that I got from place to place. God was in the lead of both our lives. Only He knows what our next steps will be, but He also knows where we are going. He sees the whole picture and how every simple step of obedience on our part keeps us on the path He has prepared for us.

Bobby and I had a lot of fun as we climbed down steep terrain, trampled over bushes with sticky thorns, and waded across streams. Since it rained often, many of the places we had to climb were very slippery. More than a few times I reached the top of a hill, only to slide all the way back down. I promised God I would enjoy myself as long as I didn't see any snakes. I even taught Bobby some hymns, which we sang at the top of our lungs. It was fun when we turned the trip into an adventure, which is really what it was anyway.

Every so often we would enter a clearing, and we could see for miles. It was so beautiful! On one side you could see the brilliant blue ocean and feel the refreshing breeze. On the other were lush, green, rolling hills covered with coconut trees. My treat came when Bobby climbed up one of the buko trees and dropped a couple of coconuts. It was always so refreshing to drink the fresh juice after walking so long in the hot sun.

During a rest stop on our way to Mr. Pann's village, Bobby began to share with me a little about his family. His mother had single-handedly raised him and his four siblings. His father had been a drunkard and left them all when Bobby was very young. His older brother Tijo had recently gone to Manila to get work to try to support the family. Tijo somehow got involved with drugs and had been brutally murdered.

"My life has not been easy at times," Bobby said as he gazed out over the valley. "God has now given me the strength to reach deep inside of myself and know He is with me. I do not think about what I do not have or how hard life is; I like to think about what I do have. I have the best thing that anyone could ever want, the only thing that matters when life is over: I have eternal life. That is why I like to be your companion to the other islands—because I want to tell everyone what I now know to be true."

Bobby's mother supported this sentiment. She had decided to take over the role of breadwinner instead of insisting that Bobby do so. I think that with the death of her first son and the transformation of this one she became convinced that eternal truths and the family's participation in sharing them would do much more to sustain her family. I believed the light of such believers would take my vision for this region around this next bend in the river to the island of Madras.

Although Madras had no running water or electricity, it made up for it with its beautiful, green, and lush vegetation. The island was covered with nipa huts that housed as many as ten people in each one-room hut. The population was fairly large for the size of the island. Bobby found out quickly where Mr. Pann lived and sent a messenger right away to see if we could pay him a visit. We waited at the top of a hill that overlooked the entire island. *If we could win his favor, we could win this whole island*, I thought. Just then we saw the messenger run up the hill.

"Mr. Pann is waiting for you," he said. "Follow me." Bobby and I were so excited!

When we arrived, Mr. Pann was waiting for us in front of his hut. He prepared a bench and table for us to sit at. The table was covered with fresh coconut and other fruits. Mr. Pann gestured for us to sit down. We introduced ourselves, and he responded to us warmly.

"Mr. Pann," I said, "I respect your position as barrio captain of this island. I am here to ask your permission to set up a station for people who need health care. I have basic ointments and bandages that fight infections from insect bites. I also have basic medicines that can help with fevers, coughs, and other things that can hurt the people on your island."

Mr. Pann smiled and said, "I wondered who you were and your purpose for living among our people. I was unsure about talking to you before. The witch doctor says you are from the bad spirits, but now that I have met you, I do not believe that. There has been talk that you wanted to help Rosselle but that the witch doctor said no. I think you should have been able to help her... You are different to my people. They do not know what to think of you. But I will tell them you have my permission to help the people. I will tell them they can come to you with no fear."

Incredible peace and joy flooded my soul. It was one of those moments when you know God has opened a door and is standing there with a big smile as He watches you walk through. Although hesitant to push my luck since we were off to such a good start, I felt led to ask one more question.

"Mr. Pann, I am so thankful I will be able to help your people with their physical needs, but I would also like to help them with their spiritual needs. Would you give me permission also to teach your people how to know God and be free from their fear?"

Mr. Pann paused for a minute and gave me a puzzled look. Then he said, "You can do that, but you must start with me so they do not know more than I do."

For three more hours, I clearly explained the salvation message. Mr. Pann was very eager to listen. He soaked up the message like a sponge. When I asked him if he would like to pray with me, he said he did. He asked Jesus to come into his heart right there.

When we were done praying, he said, "I want you to make sure you tell the people how to be born again. That is the best part!"

"It would be my honor," I said, smiling.

I felt as though God had taken a big key and reached down to open the iron gates that had kept this island a prison. I am sure Rosselle was right beside Him as He did so and was rejoicing that we had been given the right to teach each person how to be free.

Bobby and I went to the island of Madras three times a week. We established a Bible study group that met once a week at Mr. Pann's home. We also planned to go from hut to hut to share with the people "how to be born again," and we set up a first-aid station for people to come to us during certain times.

Word spread quickly that Mr. Pann had the Americana at his home to learn about the Bible. When we came the following week, about thirty men had come because Mr. Pann had told them to. This had been our prayer all along—to reach the men. If the men understood and became believers, we would have access to the whole family. Many of the youth and women were given a hard time for engaging in anything without the men's approval.

We gave each man a Tagalog Bible. When we returned the next week, we found that many of the men had read from Matthew all the way through the book of Acts. Reading the surprise on my face, Mr. Pann explained that he had told them to do that.

I laughed. "You're going to make a great pastor one day."

I often thought about the big plan God had for this area, for the people, and for me. What happened on the island of Madras made me realize that what I had thought was the plan was only a vehicle to it. God is at work causing all things, in His time, to work together for good for the ultimate purpose of shaping us to be more like Jesus. Even in our planning He is shaping us. When we submit ourselves to God, He uses all our experiences—good and bad—to make us useful to Him. He knew the steps that would follow my work with Pay Job in spite of the witch doctor's warning. He knew the steps that would follow the death of Rosselle. He even knew how the independence forged in my childhood under the fire of parental neglect would lead to the courage and determination I would need to approach this island. It was a matter of trusting His plan and obediently walking His path regardless of how far down the road I could see.

CHAPTER TEN

House of Joy

And we know that in all things God works for the good of those who love him.

Romans 8:28

So many had come to Christ from the surrounding villages that I decided it was time to bring them all together for worship in one location. In a joint effort we began construction on our first church building. Men came together from all the villages: Pay Job, Danni, Mr. Pann, Pauli's father, and Johani—barrio captains and fishermen—demonstrating what the family of God should look like and how they should behave.

Pay Job donated land in a central location, and others brought bamboo, nipa, and thick ropes from the plants in the jungle. What an exciting time! It was dry season, and the sun beat down strong and hot. As the men began to build, the women put together food and drink. We turned the whole event into a party. Long benches were brought over from the marketplace and covered with every fruit that the jungle supplied. Sticky white rice was plentiful, along with platefuls of fried fish.

On the last trip I had taken out of the jungle to get supplies, I had brought back a battery-operated tape player with worship music performed by some Filipino Christians from Manila. The entire tape was in Tagalog. While the men worked on the construction and the women attended to the food, I cranked up the music and gathered the children to sing. Before long, all the men and women joined in, and we all praised God together. We sang louder and louder with each song and began to cause quite a stir among the other villagers.

Word spread quickly that we were building a church. So many people came to help that it took only a couple of days to finish the building. The church had a dirt floor and walls made of bamboo tied together with strong ropes. The roof was a thick pile of nipa and banana leaves woven together.

What a day of celebration we had when we all came together for our first real church service. How my heart rejoiced at the sight of Filipinos from different villages feasting together, trading partners as they danced; arms hung round unfamiliar shoulders as they sang praises to God. We had a packed house on opening day, and I was privileged to give the first message in our new church building. I titled it "No Victory without a Battle, No Freedom without a Cross."

Many who had come to know the Lord before this day had entered into a whole new life. They had let go of things that had been part of their lives since they were born. They had learned to adjust from being entrenched in animistic worship to worshiping the one true God. They handled incredible pressures from family, friends, and society. They daily confronted very difficult choices. Each one had his or her own struggles. I was there to guide them and encourage them in the way they should go, functioning as a lantern in a dark place. They had needed time to adjust to their new faith in Christ and to make it their own. I encouraged them and remembered my missions professor's wise advice: "Let them make their own decisions and let them make mistakes."

On this day I encouraged the people to completely surrender everything to Jesus Christ. "He wants all of you because He gave all of

Himself for you on the cross. His was a complete sacrifice. He wants you to be a living sacrifice, completely surrendered to Him. Only then will you find true fulfillment and His perfect will for your life. He did not hold back from you. Do not hold back from Him. Come to Jesus. He waits for you patiently with open arms to take you in."

Fighting to hold back the tears, I then told them the story of a little girl who had touched my life greatly. "In another village I knew a special little girl. Her father was a drunkard and fought with the girl's mother every day. This left my little friend to wander the village streets. One day she heard some of the Christians in that village singing in one of the buildings. The songs called out to her. Realizing that the Christians came to sing several times each week, she made an effort to come for each meeting. She was too nervous to come inside, so she sat outside the building on a tree stump and just listened as the music brought healing to her hurting heart. A few people in the church noticed this little girl on several occasions and invited her to join them. The girl came, and in a short time a smile sprang to her face and she joined in singing all of the songs she had already come to know by sitting and outside listening on the tree stump. More important, she came to understand why all these people were singing and whom they were singing to. She asked Jesus Christ to come into her heart, and for the first time, this little girl felt true love.

"Only a few months later we were called to the home of the little girl. This time the father not only had beaten the mother in his drunken rage but also had beaten his daughter. Rushing the girl out of the village to a doctor in Larena, we hoped and prayed. After the doctor did what little he could do, he called me in to see her. Her little body was bruised and battered. I took her hand in mine and prayed that God would make Himself very near and present to her so she would not fear. Just then she opened her swollen eyes and looked down at her body.

"Struggling to get out her words, she asked, 'Where is my dress? My dress. I need to have my dress. Please get it for me.'

Frantically looking around the room, I noticed it in the corner rolled up in an old towel. It was torn, dirty, and bloody. Surely I could not give it to her.

"'I'm sorry, honey,'" I began to explain.

"'But'" she interrupted me, 'I want it the way it is.' Hesitantly I reached down and picked up what seemed to represent the stolen innocence of this sweet little girl. As I laid it on her stomach she embraced it with her arms and said, 'Thank you. I'm going to see Jesus now, and I want to show Him that I suffered for Him, too.' Within moments she was in His presence."

This child had found victory in her battle beyond her suffering. She had found freedom through the cross. I asked the people gathered that day, "What is your battle? What keeps you from completely giving yourself to Christ?"

I then encouraged those who had come to know the freedom of the cross to share it, share it with everyone. "What if no one had spoken to the little girl sitting on the stump listening to the music? One of the most exciting things about being a Christian is that we only need to be available; God goes ahead of us and prepares people's hearts. We cannot save people; we can only tell them how to be saved. God is the one who then will go deep into their hearts as He has done for us and confirm in our spirit that He is the way, the truth, and the life."

As I was speaking, I noticed a woman sobbing. I had seen her before at other services, but she had not yet made a decision to follow Christ. I had not pressured her, believing that God would work in her heart in His time. At the end of the service, I said that anyone who wanted to talk privately could come up to the front and I would be there. This woman came forward. Her name was Ate Fe De Guzman.

Still sobbing, she tried to explain to me what was on her mind. "I thought that maybe Jesus was just another spirit, maybe one that I could count on. I came here to learn how to have a good spirit on my side. Today I see what is true. God is the only real God, and I see now what you mean about Jesus dying on the cross for my sins. He gave all of Himself for me so that I would have a way to God. I want to give every bit of myself to God. I want to belong only to Him. I will do anything He wants me to. Will you help me? Will you help me teach my family? I have eight children, and my husband works overseas. We need to tell him somehow. Please come to my home today to talk with my children."

There was nothing more exciting to me than watching God at work in a person's heart. I marveled at the way God revealed Himself to these people. Maybe they were attuned to spiritual things through animism and that made the reality of Christ one of such clarity once they came to understand Him. I'm not sure, but the light of Christ seemed to fill their hearts in such a way that they were transformed upon accepting Him. It happened that way with so many, including Ate Fe. I agreed to meet with her in her village later that day.

Ate Fe lived in a village called Balkan, which I had not as yet visited much. I walked several miles to reach her home, which was different from any other home I had seen in the villages. Her husband, Rudy, had sent money and supplies to build a home out of materials that were not easy to come by in the jungle. The home was made mostly out of wood and some sort of drywall inside, but parts of it were made of bamboo and nipa. It had one big open room that they called their restaurant. Behind it were three other rooms, one for cooking and the other two for sleeping.

What shocked me most was the big jukebox at the back of their restaurant. The jukebox was run by a generator and blasted all sorts of rock music to gather a crowd. Then the family would sell simple dishes of rice, vegetables, and fruit. This was how Ate Fe supplemented her family's income. On one wall was painted a huge mural of one of the good spirits, called Santo Nino. After I got over the shock of seeing a jukebox in the jungle, I thought, *Now I've seen everything.* Ate Fe gestured for me to sit down. Other thoughts began crowding my mind: *How did they get a jukebox all the way out here? Ate Fe is going to have to stop playing that horrid music! And she will have to paint over that hideous mural!* I took a deep breath and tried to focus on meeting her children.

Her two eldest were girls—Leah, who was fifteen, and Criselda, who was fourteen. The girls had been with their mother at the service earlier in the day. Ate Fe took the six younger children to another room so that I could have a quiet talk with Leah and Criselda. Both of the girls were absolutely gorgeous. Leah had long, straight, black hair and a sweet, very innocent and pure look about her. She was about five feet tall and thin. When she smiled, she seemed to light up the room. She had the kind of cheeks you just wanted to grab and pinch when she smiled. Although Criselda was a year younger, she seemed older. Her hair was black, shoulder length, and very thick. She was a little taller than Leah, maybe five-foot-two. She was a little healthier looking, but still thin. She seemed more sure of herself and spoke with maturity. She stood tall and seemed very proud. I wondered what their reaction was to my sermon and their mother's invitation for my visit.

We talked for about two hours. Both girls were very open to everything that I had to say. Somehow it all made sense to them as I compared God to the wind. "God is like the wind. We cannot see the wind, but we believe in the wind because we can feel it blow across our face and we can see what it does. We cannot see God, but we can feel Him when He is near, and we can see what He does in the lives of people who believe and follow Him."

The girls understood and had become ready to pray to accept Jesus into their hearts, giving Him theirs in return. I'll never forget that moment. Both girls bowed their heads and wept as they followed me in prayer. I knew that God had revealed Himself to them and that this was real for them. Both girls were very sincere. I left each of them with a Bible and a lesson plan for them to finish on what to do after you give your life to Jesus.

Ate Fe then came back and joined us. After I had answered some of her questions, she said she wanted to give her life to Jesus.

She bowed her head and prayed just as her girls had. It was a very emotional time. Something about the hearts of these women found a kindred connection in my own heart. We were all very aware of the presence of the Holy Spirit. I knew—as did they—that God had plans for them.

We talked about my coming every week to do a Bible study that they could invite others to. They had plenty of room, and they agreed to it. Another open door to another area! I silently thanked God for moving in the hearts of this family. Before I left, Criselda asked if she could talk to me. We went to another room. She said, "Next week the bones of Jose Balkon are going to be moved to a new shrine built in his honor. The entire town has been told that we are to participate in a parade for the occasion. I do not want to worship those bones. Is this wrong? What should we do? If we do not participate, we will be mocked. They may humiliate us in front of everyone. They may make us march through town for everyone to jeer at us."

I led her back to where the others were. I asked them all to read as much as they could in their Bibles, starting in the book of John. I told them each to pray and ask God to help them make the right decision. I told them what I thought but emphasized that each of them should make her own decision. I prayed with them before I left, asking that God would guide them clearly. I told them I would be back next week.

As I left, I wanted so badly to tell Ate Fe she should stop playing the loud music and that she should find a way to cover up the mural. But I could hear Dr. Albright saying, "Let them make their own decisions; let them make mistakes." I felt this was something I needed to let them do on their own. I needed to pray for them and give them room to grow.

The next week flew by with everything that had to be done in classes on the other islands, but I looked forward to going back to see Ate Fe De Guzman and her family the day after the parade had taken place. I wondered what they had decided to do. Criselda saw me coming and ran to greet me. She wrapped her arms around me and gave me a big Filipino kiss (the Filipinos tuck their lips under and touch your face lightly). She then grabbed my wrist and pulled me down the path to her home.

I walked into the big, open room. It was quiet. I looked for the jukebox, but it was no longer there. Ate Fe came out of the kitchen with a big smile on her face, followed soon by the rest of the family. She said, "We all decided it was not a good thing to worship the dead man's bones. We want to worship Jesus only."

They were all smiles as they told me how they had been mocked. They had not been made to march in the streets, for which they were thankful, but the people had all been told to mock them as they passed their home in the parade.

"I do not mind that they mock us," Criselda said, "because now they know we believe we shouldn't worship those bones. Maybe some will ask why and we will be able to tell them about Jesus."

I rejoiced with them that they had made the right decision and that they were already looking for ways to tell others about their newfound faith.

"What about the jukebox?" I asked.

"After we made the decision not to march in the parade," Ate Fe said, "we decided that it was probably not right to play the kind of music we were playing. It didn't seem right, so we were going to ask you what you thought."

I thought for a moment and realized I would soon be needing to go to Manila for supplies. So I asked Ate Fe, "How would you like to accompany me to Manila? We can purchase some Christian music in Tagalog and play it instead. We can buy whatever we need to turn this restaurant into a place of witness."

They loved the idea. We went to Manila soon after and came back ready to transform the restaurant into "The House of Joy." The juke-box now played *Papuri* (Filipino Christian music) instead of rock music. The mural was covered up with a big banner on which we had painted the Scripture verse "Delight yourself in the Lord and he will give you the desires of your heart" (Psalm 37:4). In front of the big, open room we hung another sign that read "The House of Joy."

Over time, this became the most popular hangout for all the people in the village. Many people gave their lives to the Lord there as a result of Ate Fe's, Criselda's, and Leah's witness, including the rest of their family. They were the ones who established the work in Balkan. I just showed up to teach the people who came.

Ate Fe De Guzman and her children were like family to me. For part of my time in that area, I lived with them. Criselda and Leah became like sisters to me. The entire family was and will always be very dear to my heart. As I look back, it seems especially right that the first meeting in our newly built house of God led to "The House of Joy."

Chapter Eleven

Burning Bibles

If a man remains in me and I in him, he will bear much fruit.
John 15:5

Butch was one of the young boys in the village. He had once been a big troublemaker, but God had turned him around. After becoming a Christian, Butch was still causing trouble, but trouble of a different kind—he began making trouble for the enemy. Butch went to all of his friends and told them about Jesus. He'd basically bully them to church, and then Danni or Bobby would take over.

Butch brought Jun Jun to church one week. Afterwards, Jun Jun came to talk with me. "I want to be a Christian," he said. "I want to follow Jesus. I lived in Manila when I was younger, and I heard about Jesus, but I never knew that He died for me until today. I never understood why people said that He is the only way. Now I understand, and I want to give Him my life."

We sat at the front of the church and bowed our heads in prayer. Jun Jun was changed from then on, and there was no holding him back. Before he left, I gave him his own Bible. He said he was going to tell his family about Jesus. We said good-bye and agreed to meet at the stage-one discipleship class the next day.

Butch came up to me after the service and said we should pray for Jun Jun because his father was one of the biggest opponents to what we were doing. I wasn't worried. I hoped the voice of a son would soften the man's heart and reveal the truth. The next day Jun Jun came to the class and acted as though everything was fine. When we asked him how it went, he said that his family was not excited about his decision for Christ but that they would get used to it. Before I began the lesson, Jun Jun asked if he could have another Bible. Without wondering why he had made the request, I gave him another one.

This boy had more zeal than I had ever seen in someone his age. He was ready to conquer the world. Jun Jun never missed coming to church, Bible studies, discipleship classes, or hut-to-hut evangelism. He always wore a smile. His eyes seemed to be lit with a flaming fire and stood out all the more because of his buzz haircut. You could just see the enthusiasm radiate from his five-foot-tall, thin frame. Jun Jun was always the first to volunteer if someone needed help, no matter what kind of help was needed. He had a heart of gold.

One day we were in the middle of a Bible study in the church building when Jun Jun's father, Mr. Defeo, stormed into the building in a rage. He grabbed Jun Jun, pulling him out of the building. Some of the older men tried to calm him, but they were not able to do so. Jun Jun's father dragged him by the shirt all the way to their hut, which was about a five-minute walk from the church.

The older men followed them to their hut but were unable to get through to Mr. Defeo, who, obviously drunk, screamed at them. "I do not want my son to be meeting with devils! I told him not to go to your meetings, and now he will pay for it again." Then he threw Jun Jun's Bible in the fire that was burning the trash. I had given Jun Jun so many Bibles, I had lost count. I had assumed he had been giving them away. Now I knew the truth.

We all met back in the church building. What should we do? What *could* we do? We all prayed that God would protect Jun Jun and change the heart of his father. I thought of Jesus' prayer in John 17:15: "My prayer is not that you take them out of the world but that you protect them from the evil one."

We prayed that God would give Jun Jun courage to endure hardship. But in my heart I wondered why these little ones had to suffer. It did not seem fair. I couldn't sleep that night. I felt responsible. Why hadn't I known what was going on? Had I been too busy to notice the signs of abuse, the subtle nuances of mood that might have clued me in? I felt sick to my stomach and was determined to make sure that this wouldn't happen again.

I woke up early the next morning, hardly having slept at all. I opened my Bible and continued where I had left off: "Fear not, for I have redeemed you; I have summoned you by name; you are mine. When you pass through the waters, I will be with you; and when you pass through the rivers, they will not sweep over you. When you walk through the fire, you will not be burned; the flames will not set you ablaze" (Isaiah 43:1–2). I asked God to please protect all those who had given their lives to Him. For those who were going to have to go through difficult times, I prayed that they would be strong and courageous and not lose heart. I prayed that somehow they would see that God would use even their suffering to form them in the image of Christ.

After lunch, Butch came running over to tell me that Jun Jun wanted to meet with me by the sea. His father had gone to another village, but they were afraid that someone would tell Mr. Defeo if they saw Jun Jun near the church building. I grabbed my bag and took off running with Butch all the way to the sea. Jun Jun was there waiting for me. As soon as I saw him I burst into tears. His face was black and blue. His lips and eyes swollen. He'd taken a bad beating.

"I'm sorry, Jun Jun," I said through my tears.

Jun Jun looked up at me as though unhurt and said, "I should have told you the truth. My father has been beating me every time he found out I was at a meeting. Every time he found my Bible, he would throw it into the fire and then give me a beating. I was able to hide it because he usually beat only my back. I cannot stop coming, because I have to keep learning. I will not give in. Jesus did not quit when it was tough. He endured more for me than I can ever endure for Him."

"Jun Jun," I said, humbled yet hopeful, "I cannot allow you to come to church without your father's permission. It is too dangerous for you, and it is not honoring to your father. We will think of another plan."

We decided that Butch would meet with Jun Jun on the side, somewhere that was not associated with the church. I prepared lessons for Butch and Jun Jun to do together. I missed teaching Jun Jun myself, but I knew this was right and was encouraged by their consistency and depth of growth. They met a couple of times a week. Jun Jun still remained enthusiastic, even in the midst of such a trial. He truly looked at the situation as a challenge, not as a burden. This worked well for about two months.

By then it was getting close to the end of the year, and my birthday was approaching. When the day arrived, I spent it working on the island of Madras. After a long journey home, I was greeted by a handful of children who escorted me into the church building. As soon as I stepped in, everyone shouted, "Happy Birthday!"

The building was packed with people from all over. They had even made a cake. I looked around the building at all those who had traveled quite a distance to celebrate with me. There were so many. I thought about what a beautiful family this was that God had brought together, but I silently wished that Jun Jun could be there. I was sorry that he could not enjoy the fellowship that he loved so much.

After cake, the guests all wanted me to open some gifts that they had made for me. I opened a beautiful picture of the Philippines that a girl named Maggie had drawn. As I looked up to thank her, I saw Jun Jun walk in. My heart ached for him. I so wanted him to stay but could not allow it. It was not safe.

Jun Jun came up to me, handed me a package, and said, "Thank you, Ate Christina, for coming here to help me. I know I cannot stay, but I wanted to give you a gift in person. I made it just for you." He was so strong and so kind. As he turned to leave, everyone said good-bye to him.

As soon as Jun Jun walked out the door, we heard a loud noise and Jun Jun scream. I ran outside just in time to see Mr. Defeo dragging him off. We ran after them to explain that we were having a birthday party, not a church service, and that Jun Jun had stopped by for only a minute.

Mr. Defeo turned and said, "I know how long he was in there. I followed him. That will be the last time he will step into that building!"

Butch ran to get the barrio captain to see whether he could help. We all waited again to hear any news. Butch came back with the barrio captain, but it was too late. Jun Jun had been beaten harder than ever before. His father was drunk, but the barrio captain finally persuaded him to allow Jun Jun to spend the night at his aunt's house. They immediately took Jun Jun to her home. Jun Jun had been badly beaten and could hardly move. His family would not let Butch in to see him. Jun Jun's aunt told Butch that she would mend Jun Jun's wounds and take care of him.

Butch came back to report what he had seen. We could do nothing more until the next day. That night I prayed for God to make some sense out of this for me and the others, and especially for Jun Jun. I had taught the others to be strong and courageous, but it was much too hard to watch this little boy endure so much. I hardly slept again that night. I woke up early and took my bag over to the aunt's house in hopes that she would let me in to help treat his wounds. I thought she might be desperate for medicine and at least let me give something to her that she could apply.

When I approached the hut, it seemed strangely quiet. Where was everyone? I knocked on the door. No answer. I could see through the bamboo that no one was inside. My heart sank. I ran as fast as I could all the way back. "Jun Jun is gone! His aunt is gone, too," I cried.

The terrible thought that Jun Jun had died in the middle of the night haunted me. Word spread fast, and everyone scattered to try to find out what had happened. I felt terrible. I told the others that I would be in the church and to please come and find me there as soon as they found out anything.

I walked into the empty and quiet building. I kept seeing Jun Jun's face as he handed me the present he had made for me. It was a picture of a tree with branches that were bearing fruit. On it Jun Jun had written, "Jesus said, 'I am the vine; you are the branches. If a man remains in me and I in him, he will bear much fruit; apart from me you can do nothing.' John 15:5."

As I knelt to pray, tears welled up in my eyes. "Please, God, make him be all right!" I pleaded. Just as I got up to walk outside and see whether anyone was coming with any news, I noticed a letter on the bench. Thinking that perhaps it had been left from the birthday party, I leaned over to pick it up. It was from Jun Jun! I read: "Many years from now when we are old...open this letter again please...to remember that once upon a time there was a sinner who fought for his life...and that sinner was called Jun Jun. Please pray for me."

Just then Butch came running in. "They've taken him away! They left early this morning to take Jun Jun to live with his relatives in a faraway village where he will be far from us."

That was the last we heard of Jun Jun. I was sure, however, that that was not the last time I'd ever see him. Someday in heaven I will be reunited with him. I pray that his earthly father will join us. I also hope that some angelic scribe will have enlarged Jun Jun's painting in one of the great halls of heaven and added the names of those who joined the Tree of Life because of Jun Jun's witness.

Jun Jun's willingness to endure pain was a testimony not only to the village but also to me. Although he was only a boy of fourteen, Jun Jun had the heart and courage of a man. The burning Bibles did not destroy the fire and love he had for his Lord. I would need to remember Jun Jun's courage in the days ahead. Little did I know, but the greatest test of my faith was soon approaching.

Chapter Twelve

A Dive into the Pit

If God is for us, who can be against us?

Romans 8:31

Unlike Jun Jun, whose courage seemed to grow under tribulation, many of those who accepted Christ reached a certain place in their growth and then seemed to hit a brick wall. It was always the same problem. Fear would grip them so tightly it was as though they were pinned down under a heavy weight, unable to move. They had been raised with such a steady diet of fear from the animistic worship that for many, even after they accepted Christ, that fear controlled the way they thought and lived.

Animistic worship is the worship of spirits in nature. The people believed in both good spirits and bad spirits, but the bad spirits haunted them. In fact, in all the time I spent among these people, I heard mention of a good spirit only a handful of times. My dilemma was how to avoid criticising their culture while breaking the grip of fear that kept them from growing in Christ.

One day a woman came to me after church service and asked me to help her child. The woman's name was Mila. She had come a few times to church and said that she wanted to follow Christ. I went home with her that afternoon to see her little girl.

"Shila has had a terrible cold ever since I have been coming to church," Mila told me. "It started a couple of weeks ago and just keeps getting worse. Is there anything you can do for her?"

I lifted little Shila onto my lap. She was about six years old and adorable, like all the little girls were, with her big brown eyes and long, straight, jet black hair. I asked her how she felt.

"My head hurts, and my body feels tired," she said.

I reached for my bag for the thermometer and some medicine. As I began to undress Shila to make sure she didn't have a rash, I noticed a strange-looking necklace around her neck.

"Do not take off that necklace!" Mila said.

"Why not?" I asked.

Mila hesitated, as if unsure whether she should tell me, then finally said, "The witch doctor gave that to Shila when she was very ill as a toddler. He told me never to take it off or she would get ill again and die."

I was furious. I knew that I had to give Mila time to grow in her faith, but I was becoming annoyed by all the trinkets that were keeping these people in bondage. How could I make the people understand that Jesus had come to set them free—from sin and from the need for trinkets? For too many, fear, not Christ, was their master.

Steaming inside but trying to keep my cool, I said, "Mila, I want you to take that necklace off Shila right now."

Mila froze in fear. "I can't!" she protested. She explained that Shila had been deathly ill when she was a small child and that she didn't want to have her daughter die now because of her disobedience.

I sat with Mila for the rest of the afternoon going from Bible verse to Bible verse that showed that God would take care of her. "Since God is for us, who can be against us?" I read. "When you give your life to Christ, you belong to Him. You are His, and He will watch over you. You have to choose whom you are going to serve. Your allegiance cannot be to both God and the witch doctor. You have to make a choice."

Mila affirmed that she wanted to do what God wanted. I put Shila on Mila's lap and asked her to follow me in a prayer to commit herself and her little girl to God's care. I then put Shila on my lap and explained very simply what Jesus had done for her. She decided to follow me in a prayer to accept Him into her heart. With Mila's permission, I reached for the necklace and removed it. The inscription on the back of the necklace read, "Keep this child well until her soul is delivered unto death." Shila was completely well by that evening.

Removing the necklace represented so much more to me than just that one incident. I had been trying to find the balance between letting the people come to terms with these things on their own and yanking them off them the moment I saw them. I felt a rush of anger at the enemy of their souls, who was rejoicing that they were still being controlled by their fears. I had reached my limit on this one and felt that something had to be done.

The next Sunday Danni was going to be preaching the message. By this time I had trained the men to do all the preaching, and they were good. I asked Danni if I could have fifteen minutes at the end of the service. I titled my message "Dare to Be Different." After getting Mila's approval, I summarized the discussion she and I had had and used it as an example. I encouraged the people to put their full trust in God, not in trinkets and voodoo. I told them that they would have to decide in whom and what they were going to put their trust. Then I challenged the people to meet at the church after lunch and to bring all the items they were keeping for protection against bad spirits.

I wondered who would come and what I should do with everything they brought. I had some ideas, but I wasn't sure which would be most effective. After lunch, people flocked to the church. Soon, it was packed. They were all anxious to finally get rid of fears they

had been struggling with ever since they had given their lives to
Christ, whether it had been for three years or for three months. This
was the first time I had confronted everyone on this issue at the
same time, and the message was very clear. This was a black and
white issue. If they believed in the truth of Jesus Christ, they needed
to live as if they were *free*. When everyone had gathered, I read
Psalm 91 aloud.

> He who dwells in the shelter of the Most High
> will rest in the shadow of the Almighty.
> I will say of the Lord, "He is my refuge and my fortress,
> my God, in whom I trust."
> Surely he will save you from the fowler's snare
> and from the deadly pestilence.
> He will cover you with his feathers,
> and under his wings you will find refuge;
> his faithfulness will be your shield and rampart.
> You will not fear the terror of night,
> nor the arrow that flies by day,
> nor the pestilence that stalks in the darkness,
> nor the plague that destroys at midday.
>
> If you make the Most High your dwelling—
> even the Lord, who is my refuge—
> then no harm will befall you,
> no disaster will come near your tent.
> For he will command his angels concerning you
> to guard you in all your ways.
>
> "He will call upon me, and I will answer him;
> I will be with him in trouble,
> I will deliver him and honor him.
> With long life will I satisfy him
> and show him my salvation."

I told the people to follow me, and we all walked toward the sea. When we reached a big, open area near the water, I instructed them all to take a good look at their things. Some had brought rings, necklaces, and other jewelry; some had brought rocks, tree bark, and unusual-looking leaves. I told them to throw these things, while thinking about what they represented to them, them as far into the sea as they could. I then loudly read Romans 8:31: "If God is for us, who can be against us?"

After much relief and trembling, the people headed back toward the village. I had been debating whether I really wanted to do what I was about to do, but I strongly sensed that it needed to be done. I asked the people to walk with me to the pit, which was a large water hole about a mile long and half a mile across that had been used some years earlier for mining. Many of their relatives had died working in the pit. Over the years the hole had filled with rainwater. A stream ran from it to the sea, and the water seemed much cleaner than the sea-water, plus it was fresh. The pit was surrounded by steep banks.

No one ever visited the pit area because everyone was afraid of it. Word had spread that the water was the dwelling place of the spirits of those who had died while working in the mining pit. The people believed that if you even touched your toe to the water, the spirits would pull you under and you would never come out.

As we walked, the people murmured among themselves. "We already threw our talismans into the ocean. Why is she taking us to the pit?"

I kept silent. When we reached the pit, a nervous silence filled the air. Some of the people kept at a distance as I walked closer to the water. Ate Fe and Criselda stayed next to me the whole time. I kept telling myself that I must be crazy. I wasn't worried about the spirits, but secretly I was worried about snakes. I had no idea what lived under this water that looked so inviting from above. I asked God to please protect me as I took off my shoes and dove in.

I felt I had to do something to prove to the people that spirits were not going to devour them, not in the water or on the land.

Since the pit represented everyone's greatest fear, I had decided to prove to the people by my actions what I was telling them with my words. I decided to go for it and swim all the way to the other side. The whole time I was quoting Romans 8:31 to myself: "If God is for us, who can be against us?"

The water was refreshing, but my mind was working overtime trying not to think about creatures that were eyeing my leg for a nibble. When I finally reached the other side of the pit I decided to continue my nerve-wracking swim as an example to them. When I made it to the other side, I decided to swim back. As I looked up to wave at the crowd, I could tell they had all come closer to the shore to watch. They looked stiff as a board, frozen in place. No one said a word. Everyone just stared.

As I came closer to the shore, I could see more and more people moving nearer to watch. At first the only people there were from the church, but the crowd quickly began to grow. I'm sure someone had immediately run back to the village to tell everyone that the Americana had dived into the pit. I kept praying that God would keep me safe. All I needed was for something to happen to me while I was trying to prove a point! Thankfully, I made it safely to the edge and got out dripping wet. For a moment it was quiet, then Ate Fe shouted, "Thank you, God!"

As I looked up at the people, I said, "The spirits have moved out. When you give your life to God, you move in with Him, and He moves in with you. You abide together—you live together. When God moves in, all the bad spirits have to move out. When you give your life to Him, you belong to Him! Remember that 'the one who is in you is greater than the one who is in the world.'"

That was a day many would never forget. Afterwards, there was an enormous change in the mood of the people individually and as a whole when we met together. The people were experiencing a new freedom, which you could feel in the air. It was as if springtime had visited the jungle. A freshness seemed to be bubbling over in the people's hearts. Up until now, many had been *trying* to do what was right, but it was like trying to drive a car without any gas. The chains had finally fallen from their feet, and the people were now filled with the realization of who they were in Christ. They were experiencing God at work in their lives in a new way as they moved out in simple steps of obedience.

There was no turning back. I could hardly keep up with everyone as the work began to grow by leaps and bounds. It was as if God had opened the heavens and let loose a huge blessing. I even got word that one of the witch doctors had changed his mind about me. Since I had made it across the pit, he decided that I must be a good spirit instead of a devil. *Well,* I thought, *at least that's some progress. We will reach him soon if we dare to be different.*

CHAPTER THIRTEEN

A Narrow Escape

Do not be afraid or discouraged, for the Lord God...is with you.
1 Chronicles 28:20

I woke up to the sound of banana leaves shaking outside my window. Someone was shouting, *"Gising,* Ate Christina. *Tayo na!"*

It couldn't be morning already. I had just gone to sleep. But sure enough, it was Danni telling me to wake up. It was time to go. All I wanted to do was sleep, my body was so tired. So much had been established in all the villages that I was beginning to feel the pressure of trying to keep up. Every night I stayed up late, and it seemed that just when I had fallen into a deep sleep, it was time to wake up again. I felt like I was standing in quicksand: Every time I tried to take a step I sank deeper. I rolled over, took a deep breath, and prayed, "God, I think I need some help. I have no idea how to even go about it. Please put it on someone's heart to help us here."

Danni had awakened me so that we could get an early start on our journey to Manila. I had been thinking of finding a church in Manila to help us. Pastor Calican had consuming interests elsewhere, so I didn't know what denomination to approach or any churches that had the resources to help. Since we also needed Bibles and materials to use in our discipleship classes, I thought the Christian bookstore might be a good place to start.

Danni and I made it through the jungle by noon. My body was tired, but I was pleased that the work had grown to a point where we needed help. As Danni paved my way through the bush we sang with much conviction one of my favorite songs, "Marching On with Hearts Courageous."

When we arrived at the village where we could fetch a bus, we had doubts that the one en route was in working condition. I wasn't sure whether it could take us even one mile. Bus conditions in the Philippines had not improved during my years here. I dreaded the trips to Manila, which was why I went only when absolutely necessary—once or twice a year.

To my surprise, in spite of appearances, the bus seemed to work fine. The same couldn't be said for the roads, which were never meant for a bus. The roads were no wider than the bus and were full of giant ditches. The ride was very bumpy. With every bump I felt my stomach churn, and with each swerve of the bus I became more and more nauseated as we swerved back and forth. The bus stopped at every little barrio we came to. As usual, the children all came running with their food items to sell. They would push each other, vying for positions nearest the windows, hoping that passengers would purchase something. I usually loved to hear the children, but this time the noise irritated me. I closed my eyes, hoping the children would go away. I was so tired, but I'd had no rest with the constant bumping and swaying of the bus.

I buried my head in my hands in a feeble attempt to avoid the noise. When the bus was about to start moving again, I raised my head just in time to see some NPA soldiers get on. The New

Peoples Army had been active ever since I arrived in the jungle region. I had seen their members several times but had never had any problems with them. About ten NPA men got on the bus, and they all sat in different places. One sat directly in front of me. I noticed something different about these men from the other NPA members I had observed—they had anger in their eyes.

My body was tense as I quickly tried to figure out what to do. The man who sat in front of me turned completely around in his seat and glared at me. His piercing stares sent an icy chill up my spine. I was afraid to talk or even move; I was petrified. I glanced over at Danni, who motioned to me with his hand to stay quiet. For almost two hours, the NPA man never took his eyes off me, while the others talked among themselves in a dialect that I couldn't understand.

I could tell by his tightly clasped hands and fidgeting eyes that Danni was afraid, even though he was trying to act as if he weren't. Why was the man glaring at me? His eyes were scary looking, glazed, as if he were on drugs. I was breaking into a sweat because I was so scared, but I stayed still. I hoped Danni would know what to do, because I had no idea. Should we get off the bus? What if they took us somewhere? Should I tell them why I was here? If only he would stop staring at me! I turned my face to look out the window, trying to pretend he wasn't looking at me, but he was impossible to ignore.

The bus then stopped, and the NPA men all gathered around the driver, talking so quickly I couldn't understand what they were saying. The driver then started the bus again and headed in a direction east of where we wanted to go. Panicking, I looked to Danni for some guidance, but before he could say anything, a couple of men from the front of the bus explained to Danni that we had no choice but to go with them.

I thought I was going to be sick. I was already not feeling well from the bus ride, and the fear on top of that made me feel like I was going to pass out. I put my head on my lap and did not stop praying. *Hello, God? In case You were busy doing something else, I think You'd better pay attention to what's going on down here.* Was God going to do something? I quoted a poem by Lee Weber over and over in my mind:

NOT OVER BUT THROUGH

I came to the swift raging river
And the roar held the echo of fear
O Lord, give me wings to fly over
If You are as You promised, quite near.
But He said, "Trust the grace I am giving
All pervasive, sufficient for you
Take My hand, we will face this together
My plan is not over, but through."

At times it is easy to trust Him
And each promise shines like a light
O Lord, I am willing to trust You,
I just don't want to walk in the night.

But He said, "You can trust Me whatever,
When courage and strength are all gone
When nothing seems right or seems easy
When all you can do is hang on."

I clung to every ounce of faith I had that Jesus was walking through this with me, and I prayed, *God, if there is a way out of this, please deliver me quickly.* After the longest afternoon of my life, the driver stopped the bus at a small village to get a drink. The man in front of me looked at me even more threateningly. The knot in my stomach seemed to be twisting me in two. I was sure it gave the man some sort of pleasure to watch the sweat drip off my forehead.

Just as the driver stepped back onto the bus, Danni got up from his seat and told me to follow him. Although I didn't think I could even stand, I quickly got my bag and followed. I thought for sure they would follow us, but I kept walking. My legs were trembling as I stepped off the bus, and the ground seemed to be moving underneath me.

A tall Filipino man stood in front of us and said, "Go to the hut next to the children." He then stepped onto the bus. Danni grabbed my arm as we hurried to the hut. I thought the man would be back. We never saw him again.

We never figured out exactly what happened. When we entered the hut, Danni explained, "When the driver went to get a drink, a man came to my window and told me to take you off the bus. That is why I got up. I didn't know if I should trust him, but something inside told me I should do as he said."

A woman inside the hut said we should stay there with her until another bus came to take us the rest of the way to Manila. She didn't talk much, and we never did learn who the man was who told us to get off the bus. I wonder to this day, was he a member of the NPA who approved of my work, heard about my captivity, and hurried to rescue me? Or was he an angel sent to keep me from the hands of evil? Regardless, I cannot wait to meet him in heaven.

The woman fed us as if we were her children. Although I did not feel like eating anything, I ate the rice in hopes it would settle my stomach. The woman warned me, "You must not come into this territory anymore. It is too dangerous here. You need to stay in Manila if you do not want your life threatened again." Danni and I looked at each other. She obviously knew something, but that was all she would say.

I couldn't stay in Manila, however. I had to find someone to help me with my work and then return to doing it. I dismissed the woman's warning for the time and was relieved when another bus came by that took us all the way to Manila. We stayed with a family we knew for a couple of weeks. We had meant to stay only a few days, but I became terribly ill. For two weeks I had a fever and everything that went along with a bad case of the flu.

Pastor Calican came to see me, and the first thing out of his mouth was, " I can't believe you're still alive!" He was trying to be funny, but he had no idea how true that statement was. I certainly was not going to tell him, because if I did, he would have fought me over going back. I should have predicted that he would anyway, for he then said, "It's too dangerous for you out there. You cannot go back."

"I have to go back," I said. "I'm not going to leave them high and dry after we've come this far." I explained to him all that had been done and that we needed help.

"I will see what I can do to find you some help," he said, "but then you need to prepare yourself that you may not be able to stay. It is getting more and more dangerous every day with the NPA activity. I do not know the mountain region where you are. For all I know you are not even supposed to be there. You stay here in Manila for a bit, and we will look into what can be done."

When I finally got well, we went to the bookstore to load up on supplies. I picked up a book called *Fire in the Philippines*. The book was about what God was doing all over the Philippines. Captivated by it, I bought it and read it that same day. The connection was so strong that the story could have been my own. The story explained how the ministry described in the book had been reaching villages for Christ all over the islands. I had heard about the ministry. Carol, a friend of mine in the US, went to a church in California that was connected with it. I immediately wrote her and explained the details of what I had been doing and what we needed. My hope was that somehow we could get some help.

Pastor Calican could not find anyone who was willing to go with us into the territory where we needed help, so Danni and I headed back to the jungle on our own. I assured Pastor Calican that I would come back to Manila as soon as I could get some help. Our trip home was a safety vigil. Although we were seen by the NPA, no contact was made. With my growing awareness of danger, I prayed that God would keep me focused on the ministry at hand, that my personal safety would not become a distraction, and that my efforts and rest would be multiplied until help arrived.

One day, feeling overwhelmed by my responsibilities and unsettled about the NPA activity, I went for a long walk to pray. I hiked all the way to the top of the mountain, where I sat for most of the day. As I looked out over the valley, all I could see was coconut trees and long stretches of land between each village. The view was beautiful. The sun shone brightly over the sea, and the waves glistened as they rolled onto the shore.

I thought of all the places that God could have sent me, and I was thankful that He had brought me here. I thought about all that had been accomplished so far. Individual churches had been centrally located for people from all of the villages to attend. Bible studies had been established on each island. First-aid stations were allowing individuals to receive basic medical treatment. Educational programs were teaching the children to read and write. A nutrition analysis station had been set up at the marketplace. Tracts were being widely distributed in Bicolano on how to share the faith. An established discipleship school was training men to serve in all positions of leadership.

That day, I wrote in my journal:

I know that without times of trial I cannot grow. I must be in a growth spurt right now, because I feel greatly challenged. Lord, as I look out over this valley, it looks so big. I know that You see the needs here, and if You have brought us this far, You will continue to provide what we need. I feel inadequate to continue to meet all these needs. Here on this mountain as I look out over the work, I feel so small.

I feel as though I have taken the people as far as I can, as far as I am. If only I had a pastor to teach me, I could take them further. I have poured my life into these people, and now I feel empty. I feel I need help to go on from where we are now. Please fill me with all that I need to continue to do what You have called me to do. I need wisdom, discernment, understanding, compassion, strength, and faith. Help me to lay this burden down. It is much too heavy for my shoulders to carry, and I am sinking under the weight of it all. Please lift it from me and give me rest. I trust that I am only facing the bend of a river. Although I cannot see what is around the bend, You do. I trust that You will continue to guide us.

I began to wonder whether I should go back to California, finish Bible college, and then return to the Philippines. Maybe I should go back to California to find help to support us here. Maybe I should heed the warnings of so many people that I should not be in this area in the first place.

I thought about my life. I was only twenty-four years old. I was still so young. Would I spend my entire life here? I thought about all the missionaries I had read about who lived most of their lives with the people they worked with. I had always been willing but had never really thought that far ahead. I just took one day at a time. Would I ever get married? Would I be able to have children? I always wanted ten kids. Amy Carmichael had spent her life in India and never married. Maybe God wanted me to give my whole life to these people. Maybe I would never marry and have children. But I wanted to finish Bible college. I wanted a family of my own.

After sitting for hours, pondering the big questions of my life, I wrote: "Delight yourself in the Lord and he will give you the desires of your heart. Commit your way to the Lord; trust in him and he will do this" (Psalm 37:4–5).

I give all rights to my life and my desires back to You, Lord. Of all that my heart desires, I desire most to do with my life what Your will is. My life is not my own. It belongs to You. I made that decision a long time ago. If You want me to live my entire life here, I will, and will do so with my whole heart. I am sure that as long as I am in the center of Your will, I will be most fulfilled. I am reminded that until I give You all of my dreams, I will not be free to begin to see what You have been dreaming for me.

By the end of the day, I was reenergized and ready to keep on going. I felt I had made it very clear to God that we had needs here (as if He didn't know it already), and I left that worry with Him.

A few months later I received a response from my friend Carol:

I was greatly encouraged by your latest letter explaining your increasing responsibilities. I had to stop reading the letter twice because I was so moved by it. Thank you so much for your honesty. I really have learned from you even in such trials. It seems that no matter how great our responsibilities, Jesus always cares and provides. You can be sure that He will lead you to a resting place of renewal.

You are like a caterpillar turning into a butterfly, being transformed into something very beautiful. God is shaping you! I am seeing less of your girlish ways, although they are cute and carefree, and seeing the woman in you develop. You are rich in spirit, beautiful in heart, loving others, serious about your calling, and sincerely responsible. No one gets there without paying the price, counting the cost, and surrendering to God's will. It is clear to me that God is working in your life molding you....

It seems that it may be time for you to come home. I'll see if I can get someone to listen. I'll find help somewhere. You'll be okay. We all love you.

Your partner in prayer,
Carol

The letter left me sure that God was going to bring help. Carol and I had known each other from our days of doing campus evangelism together. She was with me the day I led Lisa to the Lord. Now five years later, although she was not with me physically, I felt she was by my side. I was refreshed to have someone talk to me who really knew me. Carol somehow broke the distance barrier and could see straight into my heart and sense what God was doing inside me. I felt a peace come over me. Although I had no idea what was around the bend in the river, I needed to keep marching on with a heart courageous, doing what could be done in His strength and provision.

CHAPTER FOURTEEN

A Stranger Among Us

He will command his angels concerning you....

Psalm 91:11

Heat and humidity blanketed the jungle. The weather forecast for the village was the same nearly every day: 100 percent humidity and temperatures in the high 90s and low 100s. The only difference was the precipitation. Today it had rained, leaving the thick jungle steaming as Bobby and I made the nine-mile hike to Larena.

Abruptly the path broke out into a clearing that was dominated by the thatched structures that served as the local market. Spread out under the makeshift tents were tables covered with the usual market wares: bananas, vegetables, cooking utensils, and candy. Chickens in cages clucked and screeched as they awaited their sale. Hundreds of people milled around the tables, creating a din with their high-pitched voices as they sought a bargain.

Market day was still one of my favorite days. The excitement of new sounds, new sights, and new faces was a bright spot in the routine my life had settled into. Perhaps today some new contacts would be made that would result in a new member for one of the churches.

In spite of the familiarity of the settings, my five-foot-five frame and golden brown hair still stood out among the teeming sea of black hair and dark skin in the marketplace. I was like the proverbial sore thumb, and on this particular day I was attracting considerable attention—though not the kind of attention one would want.

At the edge of the clearing was a military vehicle with several young men sitting in or on it. Their proud chests were crisscrossed with ammunition belts ready to supply the many rifles and machine guns they carried. These young guerrillas glared at the crowds, bringing a tension to the atmosphere. NPA presence had markedly increased in the province as it stepped up its guerrilla tactics and then retreated to hideouts here in the jungle.

"What is that American imperialist doing here?" the men asked. "Is she CIA? We do not like her here. She could be trouble for us."

It was miraculous that I had lived deep in their territory for so long without being killed. Apparently this group thought the same thing. Sensing trouble, Bobby engaged the guerrillas in conversation. He knew that what happened in the next few moments could mean life or death for me. The men asked him, "Where does this white woman live?," " Why are you with her?"

With the help of the Holy Spirit, Bobby gestured wildly and stepped a few paces away, skillfully diverting the soldiers' attention from me. I stood still, frozen by their looks of hatred and contempt. This was the first time I had seen them geared up with uniforms and guns.

People were gathering around me now. Some felt it was only a matter of time before the NPA caught up with me, the way it had with so many others. It seemed as if everything around me was taking place in slow motion: Bobby's voice slurring, the stern faces of the soldiers watching as Bobby's arms waved slowly over his head. People's faces moved slowly back and forth from the soldiers' faces to mine, straining for telltale expressions that would forecast my doom.

And then there was a hush. It seemed to me as if all sounds across the noisy marketplace suddenly stopped, and all I could hear was the pounding of my own heart.

"Follow me." The voice was at once strong and gentle. Looking to my side I saw a man I had never seen before. He was dressed differently from the others, somehow cleaner and neater than everyone else. He was Filipino, and his face was unusually pleasant. I didn't know who he was, but I knew I needed to do what he said.

He gestured for me to follow, and I quickly responded and fell in step behind him. He led me to an opening in the thick bush that surrounded the market clearing, and we started down a tunnel-like path that was unfamiliar to me, even though I had been to this clearing many times. In the background I could now hear the excited commotion of the confrontation back in the market.

The stranger looked into my eyes and said, "Run down this path and don't look back. It will take you to your village."

Obediently I began my flight down the strange path, never questioning the man's integrity or the unfamiliar surroundings. I turned to thank him for his help, but he was gone. A comforting peace flooded my entire being as I strained to catch a glimpse of the kind stranger who had appeared out of nowhere to help me and just as quickly had vanished. I ran the whole way to the end of the path, and there in front of me stood my village. This time there was no doubt that my safe arrival was due to an angelic escort. It was impossible for me to doubt the watchful and caring eye God had placed over my life.

CHAPTER FIFTEEN

A Heart Left Behind

Being confident of this, that he who began a good work in you will carry it on....

Philippians 1:6

I was awakened in the middle of the night by a terrible storm. A typhoon was blowing through, and I thought the wind would lift me right out of bed. The whole village was holding tight to whatever was rooted strongly in the ground.

This storm was particularly severe and left the entire village in shambles. The coming week we all helped each other rebuild. I told the people that the storm was like life: Troubles sometimes blow so hard you feel like you're going to be blown away. But Jesus is the tall tree with roots that go deep into the ground. He is the only way to be saved from the storms of life. He is the refuge you can run to, a reliable shelter in the storm.

It had been six months since I'd received Carol's letter, and I had not heard from anyone in the U.S. When I felt discouraged amidst the storm of demands, I remembered what Professor

125

Albright had told me once: "When God seems silent, make sure you are really listening. You may not hear His answer because He may not be answering the way you anticipated. If you are confident in prayer that you are listening for God and still there is no answer, then keep on doing what He last told you to do. God will let you know what He is doing in your life in His timing, which is often different from ours.".

Meanwhile, tension from the NPA was increasing every day. Since my arrival in the jungle six years ago I had been aware of the NPA but was fairly naive as to the real danger it posed. I had accepted it as part of Filipino culture, thinking it would be seen wherever I traveled in the Philippines. I did not realize at the time that the army was seen in other regions of the country only when it wished to make a statement, usually in some form of terrorism. The jungle was its hideout—base camp, if you will—which explained why we had crossed paths so often. The problem now was that the NPA as a whole had stepped up its public acts of violence countrywide, so more and more soldiers were arriving in the jungle daily to hide, bringing with them quick tempers and political agendas. I was never quite sure where I stood with them. At times I thought they were in favor of what I was doing with the people, and other times I felt my life was in danger. The ones I saw regularly did not seem to be threatened by me. It was the ones who were not familiar with me, were not local, who perceived me as some sort of threat. The villagers had stepped up their "safety escorts," but the ministry continued as normal.

One afternoon as I was coming home from the island of Madras, I saw one of the children running toward me. I had received a letter from a pastor in Manila. I ripped open the envelope and read:

> Dearest Christina,
> I want to inform you that I will be coming to your village for a brief visit with two other men. We have been contacted

by our missions headquarters with your request for help. We look forward to meeting you and are anxious to see what you are doing.

The pastor then asked if I would send someone to a certain town on a certain day to provide an escort to our location. I ran to Danni's home to ask him if he would be the escort, and he agreed to do it.

I couldn't believe we were going to have visitors. I was so excited! What was more, it seemed that the other two men were probably pastors of some kind. I was thrilled to have someone come and see what God had done in the lives of so many people. We sent out word to all the villages to prepare for a big celebration in a central location to welcome our visitors. The people shared my enthusiasm as we planned for a special time of worship and feasting upon their arrival.

The day finally came when the men would arrive. I wondered what they would be like. What would they look like? Who were they? I knew next to nothing about them but felt I could trust them, knowing they were sent as a result of my friend's plea for help. They arrived in the evening, hot and tired from traveling. I ran along the pathway into the village when I received word that they were here.

They looked at me strangely, and then one said, "How did you ever get out here?" I told him I would explain later, but first I would take them to a place to clean up and get a good night's rest.

The next day we got acquainted with each other. The men were kind and gentle. I learned that they were all professors from the Bible college in Manila. They were slightly stunned when I told them how I had come to be here and all that had taken place since my arrival. They were friendly and very enthusiastic about how the ministry had developed, in spite of their shock at a people of God being raised here unbeknownst to them. We spent the entire day traveling to various villages to meet the people and see the church buildings we had raised over the years I had been here.

In spite of their excitement, I was picking up a strange feeling, which I couldn't put my finger on. I wondered whether they thought I had done something wrong. They were very nice, yet strangely reserved. I noticed they would talk quietly so that I could not hear them as we walked to various villages. Maybe I was imagining it. It made me uneasy, but it did not diminish my eagerness to celebrate—which we did later that night at the church at Balkon. Danni preached a short message. We had a time of worship, and then people stood and gave their testimonies.

After everyone had gone home, the visitors asked if they could talk to me alone. We sat at the front of the church building. It was quiet except for the sound of the lizards yelping. There was a long silence as one of the men searched for the right words.

"I am amazed at what you have accomplished here," he began. "I did not know what to expect, but it surely was not this." He paused again, then said, "Christina, you are living right in the middle of the NPA headquarters. You have seen so much of them not because they are all over the Philippines, as you have thought, but because they have their base in this jungle region. They are hidden for the most part and do not like to be seen unless they are purposely trying to cause trouble. You are not safe here."

I understood their concern and replied, "I have been here long enough that most of them know me. If they were going to harm me, they would have already done so. I think they are becoming more comfortable around me. I seem to have problems only with the ones who do not know what I am doing here."

The pastor again took his time before speaking, then said, "I am going to see to it that you get help here, but Christina, you're going to have to leave. It is much too dangerous for you here. An American woman was just killed by the NPA because they thought she was a spy. She wasn't, and she was just outside Manila. The government would tear you out of here in an instant if they knew you were here. I'm sorry, but I will have to take you out of here tomorrow."

I sank back in my seat. *Tomorrow? How can this be, Lord? Here I was expecting to have help, and now they're telling me I have to leave!*

I straightened up and said, "You've got to be kidding me. I've worked with these people for all these years and you're telling me I have to leave with one day's notice? I can't leave these people with no one to help them!" I took a deep breath as tears began to well up from deep inside me. Thoughts quickly flashed through my mind; my heart was being torn from within. The men worked to convince me that my life was indeed in danger. This was not a safe place for me. My heart cried, *Since when were safety and comfort my criteria for staying? They hadn't been from the start.* The men continued to assure me that they were as concerned as I was that the proper guidance be offered to these people. My heart protested, *You don't understand. I thought I would always be a part of that guidance.*

We talked for hours into the night. It took me some time to see that this was God's answer for me. These men had come here to see how they could help, and they were right to take me out. I was being convinced in my head, but my heart was lagging far behind.

That night I found it impossible to sleep. It all felt like a bad dream. I had invested so much of my life here. I had always thought that if I were to leave it would be a decision I would make myself and that I would gradually remove myself from the work and the people. I never expected my exit to be so sudden. But as I thought about leaving, God spoke to me in that still, small voice and reminded me that my life was not my own. He was the one who had brought me here, and He would be the one to take me out. I was only a vessel that He used to accomplish His purposes for a window of time. At this bend in the river I needed to adjust myself and submit to what He was doing in my life. He would take care of the ministry. The ministry was not dependent on me.

Danni and Bobby spread the word all night that I would have to leave in the morning. As soon as it was light, I got up and began to pack my things. There wasn't much to pack. I had a few very worn skirts, some shirts, handmade barrettes, two pairs of beat-up tennis shoes, a necklace that one of the girls had made me for my birthday, the letter that Jun Jun had left me before he was sent away, a letter from Pay Job describing what God was doing in the lives of those he had led to the Lord, and the letter I had found in my Bible from Jim Albright. I packed a handful of pictures that the little children had colored in church, a picture of a coconut tree with a view of the sea that Criselda and Leah had given me, and some of the felt that we had used to make the banner for Ate Fe's "House of Joy." The last two things I packed were my audiotape of the song "Marching On with Hearts Courageous" and a beautiful, embroidered piece of fabric the women used to make wedding dresses. One of the elderly women had made it especially for me. She presented it to me in hopes that I would marry one of the village men so that I would never leave them.

How could I even begin to say good-bye to everyone? I looked out my hut to the village and thought of all the dear people here. I decided to pour my heart into a long letter for everyone to read. I walked over to the church to leave it there. When I walked in. I almost fell over in shock: The building was packed with the people from all over the valley. They had all traveled early to say good-bye. As I stood in front of them, I knew it would probably be the last time I would see most of them in this life.

"I wrote you a letter this morning, but I am so glad to see you all and have the opportunity to speak with you face to face," I said. Trying to hold back the tears, I spoke my last words to this wonderful congregation called by God's grace. "God doesn't always do things the way we would do them. Sometimes, like today, He catches us off guard. What matters most is that our lives belong to Him, and He promises to take care of His own. God can see around the bend in the river, and obviously He sees it is best for me to leave now. That means it is best for you also, for our lives are bound together. Stay close to Him and always follow Him, trusting He knows best. He has a special plan for each of you. Let Him shape you and mold you to be more like Him. Then go out to all the villages here and throughout the surrounding islands to tell everyone what Jesus has done for you! I love you all."

The pastors from Manila were wise to keep the good-byes short, or we would never have gotten out of there. The men grabbed my bags, and we started our long journey out of the jungle. With every step I wondered, *How does one ever say good-bye to loved ones?* Pay Job, Ate Fe, Criselda, Leah, Danni, Bobby, Johani, and so many others had become like family to me. I felt a shadow of the Father's longing for our eternal reunion.

We reached the top of the mountain that overlooked the valley. This had been my starting place. Here I had prayed with such zeal: "Lord, what is now darkness, please make light. Lights shining for You. May I not leave here until there is praise being lifted from these people unto You."

Now I stood in silence and took a long, last look over the valley. This was my time to say good-bye. As tears rolled down my face, I began to hear that still, small voice again. "Can you hear the praise being lifted to Me?"

Then God opened my spiritual eyes to see a portion of what He could see. I could see lights, lights that were shining brightly in all of the villages. People, young and old alike, had been reconciled to God. "Yes, yes!" I cried. I could hear praise drifting toward the sky. I could see the heavens open and hear the praise of these people lifted to the throne of God.

Epilogue

My journey home proved much less difficult than my first year back in the States. After living a simple life in nipa huts by the sea, I felt displaced. Being faced with eight brands of everything at the supermarket was confusing. I focused on speaking at missions conferences and churches to share what God had done in the Philippines. With the money I earned through my speaking engagements, I set up a college fund for those in Manila. Everyone who graduated from my four-stage discipleship plan who felt called into full-time ministry was given the opportunitys to be fully trained for four years at the Bible college in Manila.

Along with speaking, I went back to Bible college to finish my degree. After the first semester at Simpson Bible College, I began to feel restless. I had no money to my name. I was just barely getting by and had no idea how I would pay for my tuition. I was cramming in extra courses in hopes of completing my requirements more quickly, and I was constantly looking for an opportunity to go back overseas.

On the day of our final exams, the president announced before chapel that no one could take his or her final exams unless his or her bills were paid in full. I was nowhere near paid in full. Finishing school had seemed like the right thing to do. I began to question what God had in store for me. In the Philippines I had been very focused, rooted; I knew I was doing what I was supposed to be doing. Ever since arriving home, however, I had felt displaced. Setting up the college fund and pouring myself into my studies gave me purpose, but I couldn't quite settle into the routine of being back home. Now I couldn't even pay for school. What was I going to do?

When the announcement was made, two thoughts ran through my mind. One was disappointment and dismay that nothing seemed clear to me. Disheartened and confused, I thought of walking out of the building. The other thought was to pray.

I chose to act on the second thought. I asked my friend Donna Moore to join me outside for prayer. We climbed a huge tree in front of the college. We prayed, "Lord, where we see no way, we know You can make a way. This is what I feel I am supposed to be doing right now. If this is truly what Your will for me is, I ask You now to provide the means for me to take my finals." Donna and I then walked back into the building. Within ten minutes, my name was called over the loudspeaker. "Christina Di Stefano, please come to the main lobby."

I sighed. I knew they were going to tell me that I couldn't take my finals. Donna went with me. The dean of students met me in the lobby and informed me that the president of the school wanted to see me in his office. The knot in my stomach tightened. Not only were they not going to let me take my finals, I was about to get into trouble for being irresponsible.

The president of the college, Dr. Lee, was a very nice man. He traveled a good bit, and I saw him only when he spoke at chapel. I had never personally met him. I was extremely nervous as I entered his office. He kindly gestured for me to sit down.

"Your teachers have told me all about what you have done in the Philippines," he began. "I admire your courage and enthusiasm to serve our Lord. What I want to know is what you plan to do now that you are home."

I told him that I felt I should finish school, but at the same time I couldn't wait to get back on the mission field to start an orphanage for the many abandoned children in the Philippines.

"Then," Dr. Lee said, "let me tell you a story. There once was a woodcutter who wanted more than anything to cut trees for the king. One day the king gave the woodcutter a beautiful ax and told him to go to a certain forest and cut as many trees as he could. The woodcutter was thrilled to have this opportunity. He went straight to the forest and with great enthusiasm began to chop down tree after tree. He worked very diligently year after year, cutting down more trees than anyone ever expected. One day the king sent a messenger to the woodcutter to bring him to talk with the king. The woodcutter, carrying his ax, came before the king. The king then said, 'You are doing a fine job! You have done what I have asked of you. There are many more trees to be cut, but if you are going to be most effective in cutting them all, I need you now to take a rest and allow me to sharpen your ax. When you are rested and your ax is sharpened, then it will be time to go again into the forest.'"

"Christina," Dr. Lee continued, "you are the woodcutter in this story. You have worked hard on the field, and now it is time to sharpen your ax and finish your education."

Before I could explain that I did not have the funds, Dr. Lee went on, "Just a few minutes ago I received a phone call from a Christian businessman who graduated from our school sometime back. He pledged a certain sum of money to go to a student who has consistently carried a 4.0 grade point average and who might need financial assistance. He then specified that he would prefer it go to someone who is majoring in missions. I went straight to Dr. Albright to ask him who would meet these requirements. Dr. Albright smiled, then pointed out the window. 'See that girl up in the tree? I believe she is praying right now about her financial dilemma, and we are right now watching God answer her prayer.' Now, I want you to go take your finals."

Feeling overwhelmed, I thanked Dr. Lee and stood to leave. Just as I turned to walk out the door, Dr. Lee stopped me. "Oh, one more thing. I think that it will take you about two full years to finish your degree. You do that, and I am going to personally take care of all your bills here at school. That is *my* concern now."

During those next two years I worked diligently to steward such a generous gift. The counsel I received from Dr. Lee confirmed what God had been telling me personally and through Scripture. I did not have to be "doing" to be pleasing to God. Resting and studying were just what He wanted me to be doing at this time in my life.

I maintained a 4.0 grade point average, an educational first for me, and graduated with honors. The second commencement day in my life proved as unforgettable as the first. One of the professors was handing the diplomas to the students as they walked onto the stage. I was near the end of the long procession line, this time feeling very proud. My turn came to walk up, and I headed toward the professor, anxious to hold that diploma. As I approached him, he smiled at me. But instead of handing me my diploma, he shook my hand. He then turned to Dr. Lee, who was sitting at the back of the stage.

Dr. Lee stood, took the diploma from the professor, and presented it to me. Shaking my hand, he said, "I'm proud of you. Your ax has been sharpened. May God guide you from here." Tearfully I accepted the diploma and thanked him. As I left the stage, I looked inside the cover. The diploma was there. Since I had worked so hard up until graduation, I was exhausted by the time summer came. I had become like family with the Hayfords, who knew I had worked very hard and decided I deserved a vacation. They invited me to go with them to Jackson Hole, Wyoming, for ten days. It was very easy to say yes!

Since graduating, I had planned to establish a huge orphanage on the outskirts of Manila. I was still in the planning stages and thought I would go over in another six months to begin building. I had land donated to me, and lots of volunteers from the jungle would come and help take care of the children. I decided I needed this vacation not only to rest and play but also to pray for God's direction in my life and for the orphanage plans.

We stayed in a lovely cabin owned by the Brunk family on one of the most beautiful pieces of land in Jackson Hole. We spent the time whitewater rafting, hiking, fishing, boating, shopping, and eating good food. I fell in love with the mountains! On the last day, the Hayfords wanted to rest, so I took off by myself. I hiked all day, way up into the mountains, where I found some natural hot springs I had heard about. I had a blast! I returned to my car just about dark, looking like a mess from hiking and swimming all day.

I had to be at the golf course by eight o'clock to pick up Steven Hayford, who worked in the pro shop all summer. When I arrived, two guys were finishing up a round of golf, so Steven couldn't close up yet. I went to wait in my car, which was the only one in the entire parking lot. I was leaning back in my seat listening to music on my Walkman when I saw the two guys walk off the course. They were neat, clean-cut guys, but they were heading straight for the garbage dump. I saw them reach under the dump and pull something out. Then they began to head in my direction.

I leaned back in my seat. It was dark, so they couldn't see me. When they were right in front of my car, I blasted the horn and watched them jump in astonishment. I gave them a hard time for messing around the garbage dump, and they told me that that was where they hid their tennis shoes while playing golf. We all ended up talking for a while. The guys, whose names were Jim and Michael, were looking for a phone to call Jim's wife to pick them up, but the phones were under repair. I offered to take them home, since it was just a mile down the road, and they looked innocent enough.

On the way, I learned that they were brothers. Born in Alabama, Jim played the viola for the Knoxville, Tennessee, orchestra, and Michael played the violin for the Louisville, Kentucky, orchestra. I told them that I had lived several years in the Philippines and was now back in California, where I grew up. They then told me that their other friend back at their condo was also a violinist, and he had been raised in the Philippines. That was about all the information we had exchanged when it was time to drop them off. I got out of the car to help them get their golf bags out of the trunk. They thought it strange that I helped. Raised to be independent, and living as I did in the Phillipines, I was used to doing everything for myself. Being the Southern gentlemen they were, they didn't think I should be lifting anything.

We said good-bye, and off I went. As I drove away, for some reason I felt that I was supposed to know them. I couldn't shake the feeling that I had just missed something that was supposed to happen, although I did not know what it was. The men had felt the same thing. Back at the golf course, I was driving a golf cart around while Steven closed up. All of a sudden I thought I heard someone calling my name. I went back to my car, and there were Michael and Joan (Jim's wife). They said that they had come back to get a movie, and wanted to know if I would join them. I innocently fell for it and said yes. I found out later it was all a setup just to have an excuse to come back and ask me to come over. Michael had brought Joan so that I would feel more relaxed about going with them. The plan worked. I hollered back at Steven, "I met these guys in the parking lot, and I'm going to have dinner and watch a movie with them. They will bring me home later!" Steven hollered back from the shop, "Okay. See ya later!"

Steven went home and told Betsey Hayford what I had told him, and from that moment on—about nine o'clock—till I came home, Betsey was worried sick. She thought for sure I would be found dead up on the mountain somewhere, especially as it got closer to midnight and then past midnight.

On the way to their condo, I remembered their telling me that their friend Pete had spent time in the Philippines. When I was introduced to Pete, I said to him, "Kamusta Ka?" He answered,

"Mabute' at ikow?" For about fifteen minutes we talked to each other in the Filipino language while the others just stared at us as if we were crazy. I found out that Pete had spent time in the Philippines because his parents were missionaries. I told them all why I had gone there, and we all rejoiced to find that we shared a lot of the same beliefs.

When they found out that I had majored in missions at Bible school, they asked me who my favorite missions author was. That was easy—Elisabeth Elliot. I had read every book she had written up to that point that was in print. I went on for about an hour and a half telling them all about her life as told in her books and how her books had inspired me to do what I had done in the jungles of the Philippines.

Pete said, "I bet there is one book that she wrote that you have never read. It is a book for men called *The Mark of a Man*."

I smiled and said, "Actually, I have read it. When I was in Bible college, if a guy wanted to date me, I gave him that book. All the guys in school joked about it. If someone took me out, the next day the guys would all ask him, 'Did she give you the book yet?'"

Pete, Jim, and Michael all laughed. Pete said, "You're in luck here, because Michael has already read it, and I should look at least a little familiar to you."

I didn't know at first what he was getting at. Why should he look familiar to me? Then Pete said, "Think about the book. Who is it written to?

I knew the answer to that. "She wrote it to her nephew...Pete...No way!!!"

"That's me," he said.

Sure enough it was. I couldn't believe Pete had let me talk for an hour and a half about his aunt. We all had a good laugh and talked way into the night. I hadn't had that much fun in a long time. At 3:00 in the morning we all decided we'd better get some sleep.

Michael took me home. The whole way home stars were shooting in the sky in every direction in a meteor shower. We both realized something was happening between us, although we acted cordial and didn't say anything yet. But how was God going to do something if I was leaving in the morning for California and Michael lived in Kentucky? I didn't even know where Kentucky was—just somewhere over there, east of California.

When we arrived at my cabin I tried to get Michael to drop me off away from the cabin so that I could sneak in without anyone knowing how late I'd gotten back. But Michael was a Southern man, and the door was going to be the place where he'd take me. The headlights aimed straight for the door and were bright enough to wake up anyone who I hoped would be asleep. Just as I was about to say good-bye, the door opened and out came Betsey. "Where have you been? I thought you were dead up on the mountain somewhere! And who are you? Do you realize what time it is?"

Michael apologized for getting me home so late, and Betsey and I went inside. I said, "Betsey, do you know who that is? That is Elisabeth Elliot's nephew's best friend. I met them all—him and his brother and the nephew. They are all Christians, and the one who just dropped me off—I think I'm going to marry him."

I left the next morning for California. Michael called me that night. We began a long-distance courtship, and Jim Hayford married us exactly thirteen months later. As soon as we were married, Louisville became my new home. Michael and I have been married for twelve years and have two boys, ages 7 and 8.

❧ ❧ ❧ ❧

When I first came home from the Philippines in 1985, I felt good about all that I had accomplished. But I still carried one burden that I had brought home with me—he abandoned four-year-old children who were taking care of two-year-olds on the streets of Manila. What could I do about it? I made a sketch of an orphanage. I prayed about starting it in Tagaytay. I named it "The Home of Joy." I had envisioned several homes with eight to ten children with house parents in each home. The orphanage had a large area where the children could play, attend school, and learn Scripture. This was all a dream at the time, of course, as it was still not safe for me to return to the Philippines.

Twelve years after returning from the Philippines, I asked God if He could use me to do something about the desire I felt He had placed on my heart about starting an orphanage. When I finished writing *Totally Surrounded*, I realized that I could commit a portion of the proceeds from the book to the children whom God had placed on my heart.

In 1998, I went to the Philippines to see whether it would be better to start an orphanage or support an existing one. After two weeks of visiting and talking with several orphanages, it seemed like a huge task to start one, but I did not feel that any of the ones I visited fit into my vision.

With three days of my visit still to go, my guide said, "Do not be discouraged. There is one more orphanage we will visit. It is in a place called Tagaytay." I about fell over. That is where I had dreamed of starting mine twelve years earlier.

When we drove up, the woman greeted us with the words: "Welcome to The Home of Joy!" The orphanage had individual homes, with eight to ten children with house parents in each home, and it trained the children up in the Lord. The land that the orphanage is built on had become available in 1985, the year that I had begun to pray for an orphanage to be started in Tagaytay.

A Christian organization had bought the land and started the homes to take care of abandoned children. The funding that had been donated to support the home wouldrun out in less than a month. I learned that the annual budget was about the same amount that I would raise from my book sales. The orphanage is still in desperate need of funding to continue taking care of the children. It currently has twenty-eight children, and my goal is to have one hundred children within the next couple of years. The answer to my prayer couldn't have been clearer. What a joy it is to follow the dreams God has planted in our hearts and to see them come true, in *His* time!

❧ ❧ ❧ ❧

Each of you reading this book has your own story of how God first began to call you. Each of you has unique dreams that God has planted in your heart. What is the story that God is writing with your life? Have you given Him the pen to be the author and shaper of your story, or are you attempting to write it on your own?

What can you lay before the altar today and say, "God, I can give this to You"?

What are your gifts?

What are your talents and skills?

What are your resources?

How has God made you unique?

God desires to do His work through you, using the areas where He has gifted you. You can hold all of your dreams, your aspirations, and your goals with an open hand before God. You can trust Him.

As I look back on my life, I can see how God had used both very difficult times and very good times to shape me into who He wanted me to be. As I surrendered to Him, He was able to do with me as He pleased. Nothing else in all the world satisfies the soul as does complete surrender to God. Only when you lay your dreams at the foot of the cross will you begin to see what God has been dreaming for you! And it is immeasurably more than you can even think or ask!!!

Afterword

I have kept in close touch with many of the friends I made in the Philippines. The following is an update of what is happening in the lives of some of those you read about:

Bobby Aldea graduated from Bible college and is now a missionary pastor in one of the remote islands of the Philippines.

Fe De Guzman is now in Bible college. She has a heart for helping young mothers raise their children in the Lord and for sharing the gospel with all who will hear.

Rudy De Guzman, Fe's husband, is now in Bible college and training to be a pastor. He is involved with ministering to youth in Manila.

Criselda graduated from Bible college. In January 1996 she married a young man who is trained to be a pastor. They plan to be missionaries in a hard-to-reach area of the Philippines and to establish a church there.

Leah also graduated from Bible college and is married to a pastor. They minister in Manila.

Danni graduated from Bible college and is now pastoring an area out in the jungle.

Clarisa married a wonderful Christian man who is a pastor in the United States. They live on the West Coast.

Pay Job is in heaven with Jesus!

Jun Jun Defeo, at last report, was strong in his faith and attending a church in Manila.

Discussion Questions

Chapter One: Locked Doors

1. Are you aware that God is drawing you unto Himself?
2. Is there a situation or event in your life where you sensed God's prompting?
3. Describe the situation and what you felt God was laying on your heart.
4. How did you respond to His prompting (feared it, ignored it, denied it)?
5. Was there a time in your life when circumstances seemed out of control but God worked out His purposes through them anyway?
6. How did God's intervention impact you?

Chapter Two: Without a Map

1. Do you believe that God has a plan (or a mission) for your life right now? Describe it.
2. If you could condense your answer to question 1 into one sentence, what would it be? (You just wrote one phase of your life's mission statement.)
3. If you could not describe a mission statement for your life at this time, ask God in prayer to reveal more of Himself to you. (The other stuff will come.)
4. God does not give us a map and tell us what we'll find down the road in our life. Is it hard for you to trust Him and walk one step at a time in faith?
5. Share a time you were really aware of having to trust God in a situation one day at a time or moment by moment.

Chapter Three: What's Under My Bed?

1. Name some of the "little things" in creation God obviously cared about.
2. Do you believe that God knows and cares about even the littlest things in your life? Name one.
3. If you could transport some of the everyday conveniences in your life to Clarisa's home, what would they be?
4. In the Bible we are told to sing unto the Lord. What song do you think you're likely to sing when you're feeling afraid?

Chapter Four: A Way In

1. What can you do to keep your heart attuned to God's vision for your sphere of influence?
2. Is God nudging you out of your comfort zone into someone else's life for the purpose of sharing His plan for that person?
3. Think of a time when God brought a new person into your life who did not know Jesus Christ. How did you get to know that person?
4. What shared experiences allowed you a way in to share Christ with that person?
5. Do you have a friend right now who is ready to hear about the good news of Jesus Christ?
6. What is holding you back from sharing the Savior with that person?

Chapter Five: Jewels in the Jungle

1. What would be the most difficult adjustment for you to make in an environment similar to the remote village described in this chapter?
2. What aspects of life in a remote village could enhance your walk with God?
3. If you were asked to give up one of your favorite conveniences today, what would be the easiest? The hardest?
4. Has God revealed to you something that needs to have less priority in your life?
6. Is God leading you to spend more time and effort in any particular areas of your life?

Chapter Six: View from the Mountain

1. Have you ever felt pressure to conform to a group of peers even when you knew better? Explain what happened. What will you do next time?
2. How would you rate your family on a scale of 1–10 (1, not important; 10, extremely important) in comparison to the importance of material possessions (e.g., home, TV, toys, clothes, phone, car)?
3. Write and evaluate a list of short-term goals to help you focus on eternal priorities. If you're ready, set some long-term goals. (Do this with your family if possible.)
4. Refer to your answers for Chapter 2. Do your goals coincide with your life's mission statement?

Chapter Seven: Fever in the Night

1. Has God ever surprised you when you needed a word of encouragement? Share your story.
2. Tell of a time when a friend or family member made you feel special.
3. Do you know someone who trusts you now because of a need you met in his or her life in the past? How did you earn that person's trust?
4. Is there someone in your life now who seems lonely or discouraged? What is a concrete way you can "cool his or her fever" of loneliness or discouragement?

Chapter Eight: A Deadly Banana Peel

1. The Filipino people were slaves to their fears of "bad spirits." What do you fear?
2. How does your fear impact your thoughts and behavior?
3. The Bible says that "perfect love casts out all fear." How do you think God intends for us to face our fears?
4. How would you explain to the Filipinos that they have no need to fear?

Chapter Nine: Slippery Steps

1. What are some steps God is asking you to take where you can't see down the road?
2. Have you ever been in a situation that you had to trust someone else to lead the way? Did you like being in that situation? Why or why not?
3. Can you think of someone in your life who is like Mr. Pann in this chapter? Does that person already know Jesus? If not, how might you begin a conversation with that person about his or her spiritual condition?
5. Is there someone else in your sphere of influence (home, school, neighborhood) whom God may be prompting you to confront in love?

Chapter Ten: House of Joy

1. Do you think of your home as a house of joy? Why or why not?
2. Have you ever faced ridicule for standing up for what you believe?
3. How can taking a stand for Jesus Christ influence others you may not even know?
4. Are you able to still love others when they do not agree with you?
5. Can you trust God to let people in your life make decisions on their own as they begin their walk with God?
6. Would you have made the same choice the De Guzmans did with regards to the parade? Why or why not?

Chapter Eleven: Burning Bibles

1. Jun Jun displayed great courage in this chapter. Have you ever had to oppose a family member to declare your faith in Jesus ?
2. Do you admire Jun Jun's actions? Do you think his actions affected others? How so?
3. Share some examples in which you were required to be courageous as a follower of Christ.
4. Name a favorite historical example of a courageous Christian.

Chapter Twelve: A Dive into the Pit

1. Are you holding on to something in your past, present, or future that is keeping you in bondage, such as fear of some kind (e.g., fear of failure, fear of "what if," fear of rejection)?
2. Do you have any "trinkets" that need to be thrown away?
3. Are you depending on (or trusting) someone or something other than Jesus for your meaning and purpose in life?
4. Look over your answers to questions 1–3. Make a plan to be free and include a means of accountability for getting free. Share this plan with a trusted believer.

Chapter Thirteen: A Narrow Escape

1. Name something or someone you'd risk your life for.
2. Describe a time when you couldn't see around the bend in a river but you continued and are glad you did.
3. God gives us the gift of other believers in our lives to encourage and sharpen us. Whom can you thank God for right now?
4. Who has helped move you on into a bigger vision of who God is and what His purpose is for your life?

Chapter Fourteen: A Stranger Among Us

1. Was there a time in your life when you sensed God's supernatural protection?
2. Many of us have sensed, felt, or known God's love and care for us without recognizing an angel's involvement. Tell of a time when God's loving care and mercy carried you through a crisis or a time of suffering. What was it like?
3. God does choose to use us as well as angels to carry out His purposes. How can you be God's hands or feet or heart to those around you?

Chapter Fifteen: A Heart Left Behind

1. As we read in this chapter, God's timing may be different from our timing. Explain the phrase "in God's timing."
2. Describe a time in your life, past or present, in which you had to surrender your timing to God's.

3. Is there a dilemma in your life right now with God's timing that you are frustrated over? (Does He hear me? Does He care? Why don't I get an answer or a resolution to this situation?) Explain if you can.
4. Are you growing deeper in your dependence on God?
5. Describe an area of your life in which you have sensed a deepening dependence on God.
6. Are you aware of a "window of time" in people's lives where you have been invited to plant a seed or water someone's soil?

My family, year 2000: Jake, 8; Michael; Trevor, 7; and myself

Testimony from church member in first building built (1980).

Sisters; Ananda and Leah

Maggie and me (1982) preparing for service.

Bobby Aldea in 1981. A strong believer, Bobby is now a pastor and missionary in Papua New Guinea.

Scenes from life in the orphanage.

Butch and Totey, two young believers

Me, helping to care for the children, 1983.

Village family

Me holding Ananda, the youngest De Guzman, in front of the "House of Joy."

Several of us went to the pit area" after I gave the message "Dare to be different."

Pay Job being baptized

Playtime at the orphanage

Boys taking their bath

Out in the village…

Three village girls…

To schedule Christina DiStefano Davis for your event
please contact Speak Up Speaker Services
call toll free 888-870-7719

or e-mail: Speakupinc@aol.com

Update...

If you would like to make a one time donation to the
orphanage that Christina supports with her ministry, or
would like to sponsor a child, please make all checks out to:
Totally Surrounded Ministries
and mail to
Totally surrounded Ministries
PO Box 43531
Louisville, KY 40253

IAMSurrounded@juno.com

Proceeds from this book go towards funding an orphanage in the Philippines. As a result of the growth at the orphanage, we present to you an additional opportunity to help sponsor these children, many of whom have been neglected, abused, and abandoned. Many of these children would still be hungry and afraid, with no one to love and protect them, if not for the awesome work that God has been able to do through the orphanage and the generous monthly support of people like you. Your support of $25 or more will give a child a warm place to live, regular meals, medical attention, and a loving home where they will learn and experience the love of Jesus. Please join us in bringing hope to these children.

___ Yes, I would like to support one of the children with the monthly support of:

___$25   ___$50   ___$100

___boy   ___girl

___0-2 yrs.   ___2-7 yrs.   ___7-14 yrs.

___ I would like to make a one-time gift to help build more homes for these children.

___ I would like to receive the Totally Surrounded newsletter, which gives updates about the ongoing activity at the orphanage.

Name_____ Phone ( ) _____

Address_____

City_____ State_____ Zip_____

e-mail_____ fax_____

Totally Surrounded Ministries   Make checks payable to:
c/o Christina Davis   CGM
P.O. Box 43531
Louisville, KY 40253
IAM Surrounded@juno.com